Editor
Nancy Hoffman

Managing Editor
Karen J. Goldfluss, M.S. Ed.

Editor-in-Chief
Sharon Coan, M.S. Ed.

Illustrator
Ken Tunell

Cover Artist
Brenda DiAntonis

Imaging
Richard E. Easley

Product Manager
Phil Garcia

Publisher
Mary D. Smith, M.S. Ed.

Author

Robert W. Smith

Teacher Created Resources, Inc.
6421 Industry Way
Westminster, CA 92683
www.teachercreated.com

ISBN: 978-0-7439-3212-7

©2004 Teacher Created Resources, Inc.
Reprinted, 2007
Made in U.S.A.

Table of Contents

| 1750 | 1800 | 1850 | 1900 | 1950 | 2000 |

Introduction

The *Spotlight on America* series is designed to introduce some of the seminal events in American history to students in the fourth through eighth grades. Reading in the content area is enriched with a balanced variety of activities in written language, social studies, and oral expression. The series is designed to make history literally come alive in your classroom and take root in the minds of your students.

The American Revolution was arguably the most important event in American history and one of the most critical occurrences in world history. The men who started the Revolution threw off the power and authority of the British government and set out to build a new nation. They retained a bedrock of British laws, language, and culture but created a nation to meet the challenges of a diverse population living in a rugged and dangerous new world.

An extraordinary collection of leaders blended their talents and committed their lives and fortunes to inventing this nation. They exercised their collective will and imagination toward winning the war and then committed themselves to the essential compromises that created a successful government with enough power to govern but not enough to tyrannize the people. The government they created has survived world wars, economic depressions, civil war, riots, and other great crises while the nation has endured and flourished.

The reading selections and comprehension questions serve to introduce the American Revolution. They set the stage for activities in other subject areas. The writing and oral language activities in this book are designed to help students sense the drama and danger that surrounded the creation of the nation. Students should acquire a feel for the urgency of events and the cultural milieu of the times. The research activities are intended to bring students literally into the lives and battles of people as diverse as George Washington and George Rogers Clark, Abigail Adams and Deborah Sampson, the Marquis de Lafayette, and Thomas Jefferson. The culminating activities aim to acquaint students with the life and times of people in the new nation.

Enjoy using this book with your students, and look for other books in this series.

Teacher Lesson Plans for Reading Comprehension

The American Colonies Before the Revolution

Objective: Students will demonstrate fluency and comprehension in reading historically based text.

Materials: copies of The American Colonies Before the Revolution (pages 8 and 9); copies of The American Colonies Before the Revolution Quiz (page 28); additional reading selections from books, encyclopedias, and Internet sources for enrichment

Procedure

1. Reproduce and distribute The American Colonies Before the Revolution (pages 8 and 9). Encourage students to underline as they read, make notes in the margins, list questions, and highlight unfamiliar words.

2. Assign the reading as classwork or homework.

3. As a class, discuss the following questions or others of your choosing.

   • Why do you think so many religious dissenters settled in the American colonies?

   • What are some of the variations of climate, population, occupation, and location that made the colonies so different?

   • What are some ways in which the colonies were similar?

Assessment: Have students complete The American Colonies Before the Revolution Quiz (page 28). Correct the quiz together.

The Causes of the War

Objective: Students will demonstrate fluency and comprehension in reading historically based text.

Materials: copies of The Causes of the War (pages 10–13); copies of The Causes of the War Quiz (page 29); additional reading selections from books, encyclopedias, and Internet sources for enrichment

Procedure

1. Reproduce and distribute The Causes of the War (pages 10–13). Encourage students to underline as they read, make notes in the margins, list questions, and highlight unfamiliar words.

2. Assign the reading as classwork or homework.

3. As a class, discuss the following questions or others of your choosing.

   • What were the primary causes of the American Revolution?

   • Which British act do you think was the greatest single cause of war?

   • What would you have done if you lived in the colonies during these times?

   • Should the British have imposed taxes on the colonies?

Assessment: Have students complete The Causes of the War Quiz (page 29). Correct the quiz together.

Teacher Lesson Plans for Reading Comprehension *(cont.)*

American Revolutionary Leaders

Objective: Students will demonstrate fluency and comprehension in reading historically based text.

Materials: copies of American Revolutionary Leaders (pages 14–16); copies of American Revolutionary Leaders Quiz (page 30); additional reading selections from books, encyclopedias, and Internet sources for enrichment

Procedure

1. Reproduce and distribute American Revolutionary Leaders (pages 14–16). Encourage students to underline as they read, make notes in the margins, list questions, and highlight unfamiliar words.

2. Assign the reading as classwork or homework.

3. As a class, discuss the following questions or others of your choosing.

   • Who do you think was the most important American leader during the Revolutionary era? Why?

   • Why was Sam Adams so important before the American Revolution?

   • Which leader do you most admire? Why?

Assessment: Have students complete American Revolutionary Leaders Quiz (page 30). Correct the quiz together.

Revolutionary Soldiers

Objective: Students will demonstrate fluency and comprehension in reading historically based text.

Materials: copies of Revolutionary Soldiers (pages 17–19); copies of Revolutionary Soldiers Quiz (page 31); additional reading selections from books, encyclopedias, and Internet sources for enrichment

Procedure

1. Reproduce and distribute Revolutionary Soldiers (pages 17–19). Encourage students to underline as they read, make notes in the margins, list questions, and highlight unfamiliar words.

2. Assign the reading as classwork or homework.

3. As a class, discuss the following questions or others of your choosing.

   • Who was the most interesting American soldier? Why?

   • What personal qualities helped Washington succeed as a military leader?

   • Which military leader or soldier would you have liked to know?

Assessment: Have students complete Revolutionary Soldiers Quiz (page 31). Correct the quiz together.

Teacher Lesson Plans for Reading Comprehension *(cont.)*

The Declaration of Independence

Objective: Students will demonstrate fluency and comprehension in reading historically based text.

Materials: copies of The Declaration of Independence (pages 20 and 21); copies of The Declaration of Independence Quiz (page 32); additional reading selections from books, encyclopedias, and Internet sources for enrichment

Procedure

1. Reproduce and distribute The Declaration of Independence (pages 20 and 21). Encourage students to underline as they read, make notes in the margins, list questions, and highlight unfamiliar words.

2. Assign the reading as classwork or homework.

3. As a class, discuss the following questions or others of your choosing.

   • Why did the American colonies need a Declaration of Independence?
   • Was Jefferson a good choice to write the first draft of the declaration? Why or why not?
   • Should the United States have declared independence from Great Britain? Why or why not?

Assessment: Have students complete The Declaration of Independence Quiz (page 32). Correct the quiz together.

Revolutionary War Battles

Objective: Students will demonstrate fluency and comprehension in reading historically based text.

Materials: copies of Revolutionary War Battles (pages 22–25); copies of Revolutionary War Battles Quiz (page 33); additional reading selections from books, encyclopedias, and Internet sources for enrichment

Procedure

1. Reproduce and distribute Revolutionary War Battles (pages 22–25). Encourage students to underline as they read, make notes in the margins, list questions, and highlight unfamiliar words.

2. Assign the reading as classwork or homework.

3. As a class, discuss the following questions or others of your choosing.

   • Why was the Battle of Saratoga so important?
   • What were the problems faced by American soldiers at Valley Forge?
   • Which was the most important battle of the Revolution described on these pages? Give your reasons.

Assessment: Have students complete Revolutionary War Battles Quiz (page 33). Correct the quiz together.

Teacher Lesson Plans for Reading Comprehension *(cont.)*

Victory, Peace, and Aftermath

Objective: Students will demonstrate fluency and comprehension in reading historically based text.

Materials: copies of Victory, Peace, and Aftermath (pages 26 and 27); copies of Victory, Peace, and Aftermath Quiz (page 34); additional reading selections from books, encyclopedias, and Internet sources for enrichment

Procedure

1. Reproduce and distribute Victory, Peace, and Aftermath (pages 26 and 27). Encourage students to underline as they read, make notes in the margins, list questions, and highlight unfamiliar words.

2. Assign the reading as classwork or homework.

3. As a class, discuss the following questions or others of your choosing.

   - How did the victory at Yorktown lead to peace?

   - What do you think were some of the costs of the war that were not mentioned in the article?

   - How would the war have affected people and the community?

   - Why were the French so important to American victory in the Revolution?

Assessment: Have students complete Victory, Peace, and Aftermath Quiz (page 34). Correct the quiz together.

The American Colonies Before the Revolution

The 13 American colonies that revolted against the British government were located along the eastern edge of the North American continent. Bordered by the Atlantic Ocean on one side and the Appalachian Mountains on the other, these separate colonies had each developed deeply individual political and social cultures. They had occasionally worked together on matters of common defense against Native American uprisings or threats from foreign powers, such as the French and the Spanish. However, the colonies still perceived themselves as separate and independent from each other. Their long pre-war conflicts with Great Britain over taxes, trade, emigration to the western frontier, and control of their own political institutions would help forge the birth of a united nation.

The New England Colonies

The first English settlements in New England were in the colony of Massachusetts. The Pilgrims founded the Plymouth community on the Massachusetts coast in December 1620. Another group of Puritans founded the Massachusetts Bay Colony in 1630. Despite extreme privations and the loss of many lives in the first years, these Puritans settled 130 communities by the mid-1600s. The colony of Rhode Island was created by religious dissidents who did not approve of Puritan religious practices or the mistreatment of Native Americans. Another group of dissidents founded Connecticut in the 1630s.

New Hampshire, which was settled by religious dissidents, farmers, fishermen, and traders, became a separate colony in 1680.

The New England colonists engaged in several bitter wars with Native American tribes. People in the New England colonies took over the land and gradually killed or pushed the native people off their land. They cleared land for farms and established towns occupied by craftsmen who made everything from barrels and baskets to axes and plows. These hardy New England settlers survived bitter cold winters, famines, epidemics, wars, and deep personal and political conflicts over religion.

Boston, the largest city in the New England colonies, was a very successful seaport with over 16,000 residents and many craftsmen, newspapers, and businesses. To a large extent, New England citizens ran their own political affairs through the legislatures they elected. They were accustomed to being independent of direct British oversight, and they were not willing to curtail their liberties or their independent ways of thinking and acting.

The American Colonies Before the Revolution *(cont.)*

The Middle Atlantic Colonies

The Middle Atlantic colonies were settled by other Europeans. The Dutch founded New Netherland in the 1620s, and Sweden started several settlements in what is now Delaware and New Jersey. The Dutch were forced to surrender New Netherland to a British naval force in 1664, and it was renamed New York. Portions of the southern half of this area were given to English landlords, who named their settlement New Jersey. Pennsylvania was founded in 1681 by William Penn, who was given the land by his friend the king of England to repay a debt. Penn intended the colony to become a haven for Quakers, a group of religious dissenters who disapproved of the Church of England. A section of Pennsylvania split off to become Delaware. Many German and Scotch-Irish immigrants settled in the middle colonies along with the Dutch, Swedes, and English immigrants.

The Middle colonies prospered because they had fertile soil. Farmers shipped wheat, farm animals, and other crops to New York and Philadelphia, the two largest cities, for sale overseas. These two cities used their seaports to develop thriving trading and shipping businesses. Many crafts and small industries developed in these colonies. New York City and Philadelphia had over 25,000 citizens and were the largest cities in the English colonies.

The Southern Colonies

The first permanent English settlement in North America was founded at Jamestown, Virginia, in 1607. After several years of severe famine, Indian warfare, and failure, this colony survived and flourished. Lord Baltimore founded Maryland as a refuge for Catholics, who were political dissidents in England, and to make a fortune in the tobacco business. Carolina was founded as a business venture in 1663. Political disputes caused it to split into two colonies in 1729. Georgia was founded as a refuge for dissident religious groups and debtors, who were allowed to leave prison in Britain and start new lives in the colonies.

All of the southern colonies were devoted primarily to large-scale agriculture, which included growing cash crops such as tobacco, rice, and indigo (a plant that produces a bright blue dye). The labor-intensive nature of farming in the south led to the development of large plantations owned by rich landowners and worked by imported black slaves.

The Causes of the War

The American Revolution was the result of a series of disputes between the American colonists and the government of Great Britain. Probably no one cause would have brought about the conditions for revolution. When added together, however, many colonists gradually reached the point where they felt the need to overthrow British rule and govern themselves.

Land

American colonists living on or near the frontier had willingly joined the British soldiers in fighting the French and Indian War, an extension of the global Seven Years' War between France and England. These colonists wanted the territory in the Ohio River Valley to be opened up for settlement. They saw the Native Americans and their French allies as impediments to this. After the British won the war and control of these territories, the colonists were angered when the British government issued the Proclamation of 1763, which forbade colonial settlements in these areas. The British wanted to avoid conflicts between Native Americans and settlers.

Taxes

The Seven Years' War between France and Britain had cost the British government huge sums of money and plunged the nation into debt. The English felt that many of these costs had been incurred while defending the American colonies against French troops and their Indian allies. Although they did not necessarily expect the Americans to pay off the war debts, they did want the colonists to bear the costs of stationing British soldiers along the western frontier.

Sugar Act

In 1764 the British Prime Minister, George Grenville, devised a special colonial tax on sugar, coffee, and wine imported from Britain to raise revenue. There had been British taxes before on molasses, for example, but many Americans had simply avoided payment or smuggled in the goods. Grenville decided to send custom officials to the colonies to collect the tax. American colonists led by the Sons of Liberty, a secret organization of colonists opposed to British taxes and later to British control of the colonies, decided to boycott sugar until the tax was removed. They argued that as British citizens they should not have to pay taxes because they had no representation in Parliament and their own colonial assemblies had not passed the tax. "No taxation without representation" became a battle cry for the revolt against British taxes.

The Causes of the War *(cont.)*

Stamp Act

The British were incensed over the sugar boycott so Grenville pushed the Stamp Act through Parliament in 1765. This was a tax on every paper product sold in the colonies. Newspapers, playing cards, books, pamphlets, and similar materials were taxed to support the troops. In addition, Parliament passed the Quartering Act, which required colonists to house and feed soldiers stationed in their communities if barracks were not available.

Committees of Correspondence

The anger of the American colonists was regularly inflamed by radical leaders who kept each other informed through letters. Although mail service was very slow in the colonies due to the long distances and poor roads, these committees managed to keep each other and their communities informed of British acts and the resistance of Americans in other colonies. The leader of the Sons of Liberty and organizer of the Committees of Correspondence was Samuel Adams, who became known as the "Father of the American Revolution." The resistance and boycotts organized by these groups led to the canceling of the Stamp Act.

Townshend Acts

The British were determined to raise taxes and assert their authority over the increasingly defiant, independent Americans. The Declaratory Act was passed, stating that they had the right to make laws for the colonists in all instances. They soon followed up with the Townshend Acts in 1767, which were a series of taxes on paper, paint, lead, glass, and especially tea, the beverage of choice for both Americans and Englishmen of that day. The colonists immediately began to boycott these products. As with previous boycotts, British merchants complained because they were losing business. In 1768 British warships arrived in Boston harbor carrying two regiments of seasoned troops to maintain order and support the British tax collectors.

The Causes of the War *(cont.)*

Boston Massacre

The British had 4,000 troops stationed in Boston, the center for resistance to British taxes and British authority. It was home to Samuel Adams and many of the Sons of Liberty. The boycotts were especially effective in this city of 16,000 residents. In 1770 a lone British soldier guarding the Customs House, where taxes were paid, was harassed and badgered by members of the Sons of Liberty and local toughs. He called for reinforcements, who were promptly assaulted by the mob with fists, sticks, and flying chunks of ice. A soldier fell, his weapon discharged, and other British soldiers fired on the mob. Five American rioters were killed in the incident.

Samuel Adams and his allies quickly dubbed the event a "massacre," and public anger at the British was inflamed even more. Paul Revere published an engraving of the event showing British soldiers firing on peaceful, unarmed citizens.

Boston Tea Party

The removal of some British troops from the city of Boston helped calm passions, but the radicals kept the pressure on. British leaders were determined to reestablish control over the colonies, and the young King George III was irate at the rebellious behavior of the Americans.

In May of 1773, the British government granted a complete monopoly over the sale of tea to the British East India Company. The tea was not going to be taxed in the colonies and would actually cost less than tea sold in Britain. On the surface it looked like a good deal, but it would put virtually all American tea sellers out of business.

Sam Adams, Paul Revere, and John Hancock encouraged residents to take action, and they did. Soldiers in the local militia refused to let the tea be unloaded. Adams and his allies tried to make the British tea agents quit. Adams also tried to convince the governor to send the tea back to England, which had been done in some other American ports. The king had ordered the tea in Boston harbor to be unloaded by British soldiers. This was scheduled for December 17, 1773. On the evening of December 16, however, the Sons of Liberty and local toughs dressed up as Mohawk Indians, boarded the British ship carrying the tea, and dumped all 342 cases of tea into the harbor.

The Causes of the War *(cont.)*

Intolerable Acts

The Boston Tea Party made British authorities furious. They immediately passed a series of laws to punish the city of Boston and reestablish control. These Intolerable Acts, as the colonists named them, banned town meetings in Boston, closed the port of Boston until the tea was paid for, and stationed troops in Boston where citizens had to house and feed them. Closing the port put a lot of citizens out of work and threatened the city with starvation because much of the city's food supplies came by ship. A new governor of Massachusetts was also appointed with broad powers to run the affairs of the colony, and the Massachusetts legislature had its powers severely curtailed.

First Continental Congress

People throughout the colonies quickly rallied to Boston's support. They staged tea parties of their own and sent food and supplies to Boston. In the fall of 1774, 12 colonies sent representatives to a meeting in Philadelphia to protest the Intolerable Acts. This First Continental Congress passed a declaration of the colonists' rights, which restated their rights as British citizens. They also pledged to boycott British goods and to avoid selling their products to Britain. They wrote a letter of grievance to the king, who refused to read it. People throughout the colonies began to stockpile guns and ammunition and to organize militias, groups of citizen soldiers ready to fight in an emergency. The country was primed for war, but the fuse was lit in Boston.

Lexington and Concord

In February 1775, Parliament declared that the colony of Massachusetts was in open rebellion. The declaration was passed to make it easier to arrest some of the leaders and to shoot troublesome colonists during disturbances. The British government sent secret orders to General Thomas Gage, the new governor of Massachusetts and commander of the forces in Boston, to arrest the leaders of the rebellion. Boston rebels learned of the orders, and the leaders fled the city. Gage decided to capture stockpiles of guns and powder at Concord, a city near Boston. Paul Revere and William Dawes were sent to warn the rebel leaders. The next day on April 19, 1775, American militia called *minutemen* (because they were ready to fight at a minute's notice) opposed British troops at Lexington on the route to Concord. The short skirmish here was the first battle of the war. Another fight occurred at Concord, and Americans ambushed the soldiers on the way back to Boston. The British ended up with around 250 dead, and the Americans lost about 90 in the first battle of the war.

American Revolutionary Leaders

Samuel Adams

Samuel Adams was a poorly dressed, disheveled-looking man who had accomplished little in his life. He had failed miserably as a businessman and a lawyer. In the decade before the American Revolution, however, this man in his forties would be the spark plug of colonial rebellion against Great Britain. He organized the Committees of Correspondence so that agitators and leaders in one colony would know what was happening in the others.

Adams started the Sons of Liberty as a group of radicals opposed to British interference in colonial life. This organization became a revolutionary action group increasingly devoted to complete separation from Great Britain. Adams' masterful use of propaganda in the Boston Massacre (where only five rioters were killed) and the Boston Tea Party propelled Boston and the rest of the colonies along the road to rebellion. As a result, he is called the "Father of the American Revolution."

Benjamin Franklin

In his time, Benjamin Franklin was one of the most famous individuals in the world. A highly respected scientist, Franklin studied electricity, weather, ocean currents, and various other scientific phenomena. He invented bifocal glasses, an efficient stove, and lightning rods, among many other useful gadgets. Franklin was one of the wealthiest men in Pennsylvania when he retired in his early forties from the printing business and devoted his life to public service. He started the first fire department and public library in America and helped found what became the University of Pennsylvania.

Franklin served as an agent in London for Pennsylvania (as well as Georgia and Massachusetts) during the period from 1757 to 1775. He became convinced that the colonies needed to unite and separate from Great Britain. He served as ambassador to France during the war, helped write the Declaration of Independence and the Constitution of the United States, and helped negotiate the peace treaty ending the war.

American Revolutionary Leaders *(cont.)*

John Adams

John Adams was a respected and successful Massachusetts lawyer who gradually came to support the radical, patriot positions of his cousin Samuel Adams. A powerful and effective orator, Adams was able to sway people with his debating skill and careful reasoning. He became one of the core leaders of the Continental Congress and was an outspoken advocate for revolution while many other delegates still hoped for reconciliation with Great Britain.

Adams believed everyone was entitled to proper justice, even the unpopular British soldiers who participated in the Boston Massacre. He could be vain, stubborn, bluntly honest, and politically shrewd. Adams helped write and edit the Declaration of Independence. He nominated George Washington as commander of the American army. He helped negotiate aid from France, worked as a negotiator on the peace treaty, and later served as vice president and president of the United States.

Thomas Jefferson

Thomas Jefferson was one of the best-educated men of his time. Heir to a large plantation with many slaves, he graduated from William and Mary College. A trained lawyer, Jefferson became a respected statesman, scientist, landscape artist, and architect, among many other interests. He became a leading voice for revolution after publishing a well-reasoned attack on British policies.

Jefferson served in the Continental Congress and was the principal author of the Declaration of Independence. Jefferson served as governor of Virginia, minister to France, secretary of state, vice president, and president of the United States. He helped found the University of Virginia before his death on July 4, 1826, the 50th anniversary of the Declaration of Independence.

Thomas Paine

Thomas Paine was a British corset maker who came to the United States in 1774 at the urging of his friend Benjamin Franklin. In 1776 Paine wrote the pamphlet *Common Sense*, which clearly and simply laid out the arguments for independence from Great Britain. Tens of thousands of the pamphlet were sold, and it served to convince many Americans that it was time to rebel against the British. In the darkest days of the war, Paine wrote a series of essays entitled *The Crisis*, which helped convince Americans to stand firm and endure.

American Revolutionary Leaders (cont.)

John Hancock

John Hancock was one of the wealthiest men in the colonies. He inherited a very large trading business from his uncle in 1764 when he was only 27. Although he first accepted the British tax policies, he soon became a fervent opponent to the Stamp Act and the subsequent policies of Great Britain. Hancock became an ally of Samuel Adams. The famous ride by Paul Revere and William Dawes was to warn Hancock and Adams that the British intended to arrest them. Hancock served as president of both the First and Second Continental Congresses and was the first person to sign the Declaration of Independence. He later served nine terms as governor of Massachusetts.

Patrick Henry

Patrick Henry did not seem like the kind of person to give voice to a nation. A rather lazy child, he showed little promise as a student and did not seem terribly ambitious. He failed as a storekeeper and worked with his father-in-law as an innkeeper. He received a license to practice law after only six weeks of study and had few clients. He acquired a reputation as a brilliant orator when he argued a case against British interference in American affairs. He became a leading speaker against British authority. His most famous line—"Give me liberty or give me death"—became a rallying cry for the Revolution.

Paul Revere

Paul Revere was a skilled craftsman who was trained by his father as a silversmith and later learned copper engraving as well. He became an early opponent of British policies and a leader of the Sons of Liberty. His engraving of the Boston Massacre helped incite anger at British troops and the laws they enforced. Revere helped plan and execute the Boston Tea Party and was also a courier, carrying messages to various rebel groups. His famous horseback ride to warn Adams and Hancock was interrupted by the British before he could reach Concord.

John Dickinson

John Dickinson was famous as a Revolutionary activist and author of *The Letters from a Farmer in Pennsylvania* in which he attacked British taxation without representation. Dickinson favored peace and reconciliation with England and did not sign the Declaration of Independence. Once war began, however, he served as a colonel in a Philadelphia unit. He was chairman of the committee that wrote the Articles of Confederation and later served at the Constitutional Convention.

Revolutionary Soldiers

George Washington

As commander of the Virginia militia during the French and Indian War, George Washington had been only moderately successful in battle. However, he did acquire military experience and the respect of his fellow Virginians for his efforts. Washington inherited extensive land holdings and later married a very wealthy widow, making him one of the wealthiest men in America when the war started.

Tall, powerfully built, self-confident, and having a commanding presence, Washington was able to inspire the tattered soldiers of the Continental Army to hold out against the stronger and better-trained British forces. As commander in chief of the army, Washington was often defeated, always short of supplies, and led poorly trained troops and officers. In spite of those odds, he was able to force the British to spend large sums of money to fight the war and then eventually to surrender. In later years, Washington presided over the Constitutional Convention and became the first President of the United States. He is known as the "Father of His Country."

George Rogers Clark

A major in the Virginia militia, George Rogers Clark led a group of frontiersmen to attack British-controlled settlements on the Illinois frontier. British-led attacks had put severe pressure on American frontier settlements. Clark captured a British garrison in Kaskaskia and later captured the settlement of Vincennes on two occasions. Except for the British stronghold at Detroit, Clark held control of the western frontier for the duration of the war.

Nathan Hale

A patriot schoolteacher who became a commander of a company of rangers, Nathan Hale volunteered to go behind British lines to secure essential information for General Washington before the Battle of Harlem Heights. Hale was captured in his disguise as a Dutch schoolteacher. He was carrying documents that clearly indicated he was an American spy. Hale was hanged as a spy the next day. His last words were: "I regret that I have but one life to give for my country."

Revolutionary Soldiers *(cont.)*

Alexander Hamilton

An immigrant orphan from the British West Indies, Alexander Hamilton attended King's College in New York and started writing pamphlets opposing British policies in the colonies. In 1775 he created a volunteer artillery company and served with distinction in battles at Long Island, Trenton, and Princeton. At the age of 20, he became a personal aide and close friend to General Washington whom he served as a military and political advisor. He later fought with the Marquis de Lafayette in the battle of Yorktown. He served in the Continental Congress after the war and at the Constitutional Convention.

"Mad" Anthony Wayne

Anthony Wayne received his nickname because of his ferocious skill on the battlefield and his willingness to take big chances. In the Battle of Green Spring in 1781, his small force ended up facing the entire army of British General Charles Cornwallis. Wayne ordered his troops to attack against these overwhelming odds, a maneuver which allowed most of his men to escape. He was one of the most reliable and successful American generals during the war.

Margaret Corbin ("Captain Molly")

Margaret "Molly" Corbin followed her husband John, an artilleryman, from camp to camp. When he was killed in the battle of Fort Washington in November 1776, she took over his cannon and continued firing until she was wounded and captured by the British.

Henry "Light-Horse Harry" Lee

Henry Lee was the greatest American cavalry leader of the Revolutionary War. General Washington quickly recognized Lee's superb horsemanship and superior battle tactics. In the early years of the war, Lee fought in the north with Washington's forces and in 1780 went south to battle in Virginia and the Carolinas. His hit-and-run tactics bedeviled the British units, and his daring attacks in larger battles often saved American troops from defeat, especially at the Battle of Eutaw Springs in 1781. Lee managed to squander a fortune through bad investments and gambling after the war. He was the father of Robert E. Lee, the commander of the Confederate Army during the Civil War.

Revolutionary Soldiers *(cont.)*

Mary "Molly Pitcher" Hays

Mary Hays was a cleaning woman who accompanied her husband when he left his barbering business to fight in a Pennsylvania artillery regiment in 1775. During the battle of Monmouth, New Jersey, in 1778, she was carrying water to the men when her husband was wounded at his gun. She took his place as cannon loader for the duration of the battle and later received a pension from Congress for her services during the war.

Marquis de Lafayette

Born to the wealth and privilege of the French aristocracy, the 19-year-old Marquis de Lafayette came to America to help the U.S. colonies achieve their freedom from Great Britain. He volunteered in General Washington's army and was wounded at Brandywine. Later he became a field commander and led his troops with distinction and success. Lafayette commanded one of the three American divisions that forced the surrender of Cornwallis at Yorktown. After going home to France, Lafayette fought in the French Revolution. He returned to the United States in 1824 for a tour of the nation he had fought to create.

Nathanael Greene

One of the unsung heroes of the American Revolution, Nathanael Greene was the youngest brigadier general in the Continental Army. He raised companies of militia that fought in the battle of Long Island. Later he was defeated at Fort Washington but won at Trenton with General Washington. Greene served as quartermaster general of the army for a time and helped to improve the army's supply and transportation system, despite the severe financial problems of the new nation. Later Greene commanded the troops in the southern theater of the war, where he was successful in reducing the effectiveness of the British forces under Cornwallis.

Deborah Sampson

Using the name Robert Shurtlieff, Deborah Sampson disguised herself as a man and enlisted in the Continental army as a private. She fought in skirmishes at West Point and Tarrytown and was wounded by a saber. She treated her own wound to avoid discovery. Wounded by a bullet in a later raid and suffering from a fever, her identity was finally discovered. She was honorably discharged and later awarded a pension by Congress.

The Declaration of Independence

The Second Continental Congress

As the American colonies became more and more incensed by British efforts to impose taxes and exercise authority over them, some colonists were beginning to believe that only a complete separation from Great Britain would be acceptable. The Second Continental Congress met in May 1775 with the colonies in a state of crisis. The Intolerable Acts had inflamed American anger not only in Boston but also throughout all of the colonies.

The tea parties in Boston and elsewhere had demonstrated colonial resolve to avoid paying British taxes, but the battles at Lexington and Concord had stiffened British resolve to teach the colonists a lesson. Armed men in all of the colonies organized into militias to prepare for the coming conflict. The Continental Congress attempted to ward off the impending conflict by sending a petition to King George III suggesting a peaceful solution, but he refused to even read it. In June of 1775 at the suggestion of John Adams, the Congress appointed George Washington as commander in chief of the Continental Army.

The Committee of Five

In June 1776, Richard Henry Lee of Virginia presented a resolution in the Congress seeking full independence from Great Britain. At the time only seven colonies voted to support it. Some colonies needed the approval of their legislatures, and others were undecided. On June 11, 1776, five members of Congress were appointed to draft a declaration of independence to be voted on by the full Congress. John Adams of Massachusetts and Roger Sherman of Connecticut represented the northern colonies. Benjamin Franklin of Pennsylvania and Robert Livingston of New York represented the middle colonies. Thomas Jefferson of Virginia represented the southern colonies.

Jefferson Chosen to Write the Document

The Committee of Five had several meetings and chose Thomas Jefferson to write the original draft. He was well known as a gifted writer and a strong supporter of independence. Adams was particularly blunt in his reasons for supporting Jefferson. He was a Virginian, and they needed southern support for the resolution. Jefferson was also popular and well liked, as opposed to Adams who characterized himself as "obnoxious, suspected, and unpopular." Thirdly, Adams said that Jefferson could write 10 times better than he could.

The Declaration of Independence *(cont.)*

The Author

Thomas Jefferson had long been a student of government. He had read widely about the various forms of government and had especially been influenced by the theory of natural rights proposed by John Locke, who argued that men are born with natural rights and that governments should be run for the benefit of all people, not just rulers and the wealthy.

Jefferson spent about two-and-a-half weeks writing his draft, mostly in the evenings. He had other congressional sessions and committee meetings to attend during the day. Jefferson showed his final draft to the other committee members, in particular Franklin and Adams, who made a few suggestions and changes. The document was submitted to Congress on June 28, 1776.

The Lee Resolution

On July 1, the Continental Congress met to debate the Lee Resolution that the colonies become independent of Great Britain. An official vote on July 2 ended with 12 votes for independence. New York's delegation still did not have authorization from their legislature, although it would come a few days later.

For two days the Congress discussed Jefferson's draft. About 80 changes were made in the text, sometimes changes in wording or punctuation and sometimes deletion of entire paragraphs. Jefferson, a slaveholder himself, wanted to declare an end to slavery, but some southern representatives would not accept this.

The Signing

In late afternoon on July 4, the delegates were satisfied with the Declaration and ready to sign it. John Hancock signed the document as president of the Continental Congress, and that made it legal. He wrote in a very large script, he claimed, so that King George could read it without his spectacles. The document was quickly printed and proclaimed throughout the colonies. General Washington had it read to the troops. Later 55 other members of Congress signed the document pledging their lives, their fortunes, and their sacred honor to secure their liberty.

Revolutionary War Battles

Bunker Hill (Breed's Hill)

After the battles of Lexington and Concord Massachusetts, in April of 1775, the British commander in Boston, General Gage, decided to station British troops on two areas overlooking the city. This was to ensure that British troops would have the high ground in any future engagements and also to deter colonial ambushes. The rebels had an extremely effective spy network in Boston, which probably included the American wife of General Gage, and were able to learn of the British plans.

American militia quickly scrambled up Breed's Hill and set up defensive positions as best as they could with their limited arms and cannon. On June 17, 1775, Gage ordered his men to storm the colonial positions. The determined rebels held off two full charges by vastly superior, professional British troops. Because they were out of ammunition, a third charge forced the Americans to retreat but not before they inflicted more than 1,000 casualties (dead and wounded) on the British and received about 400 casualties themselves. It was the deadliest single battle of the entire war.

The British Evacuate Boston

In May 1775, an impetuous and determined rebel named Ethan Allen had led a militia of Green Mountain Boys in the successful capture of a British outpost at Fort Ticonderoga in northeastern New York. In an incredible act of determination, an artillery officer named Henry Knox and a small group of men managed to transport 59 captured cannons from Fort Ticonderoga across more than 300 miles of rugged terrain and down frozen rivers in the middle of the winter to Boston, Massachusetts, where he supervised their placement on Dorchester Heights outside of Boston. The British army was prepared to storm the heights when a severe storm canceled the attack. Recognizing the likely cost of an attack, the British decided to evacuate Boston in March 1776 and sail to New York City.

The New York Campaign

General William Howe and his large army arrived in New York City in July. Howe aggressively sent ships up the Hudson River and landed troops on Staten Island in New York. Joined by Hessian (German) mercenary troops and General Clinton's troops from South Carolina, Howe had about 45,000 troops with which to take New York City and cut the colonies in half. Washington had about 20,000 troops—all poorly equipped and largely untrained. More than half of Washington's troops had little military discipline or experience.

Revolutionary War Battles *(cont.)*

The Battle of Long Island

Although he knew that he could not successfully defend New York City against the large number of troops his army faced, Washington realized that he had to at least try to defend the city for political reasons and because the loss of morale from not fighting would be detrimental. He fortified Brooklyn Heights, an elevated area on the western end of Long Island. In August of 1776, British troops landed on Long Island and attacked Washington's fortified positions. The British commander, Sir William Howe, had vastly superior numbers but attacked cautiously. The leadership of some of the American commanders was noticeably poor, and the American army was almost destroyed. While Howe cautiously prepared for a final assault on the colonial positions, Washington's army was able to escape. Washington lost the Battle of Long Island and was forced to evacuate New York. A second force of patriots defended Fort Washington on the island of Manhattan but was forced to surrender in November.

Trenton and Princeton

Washington's army was on the ropes, and Howe was confidently closing in for the kill as Washington retreated through New Jersey. However, on Christmas day in 1776, Washington planned a daring attack on a large Hessian force in Trenton. At dusk, he took about 2,400 men and 18 cannons across the Delaware River. They marched nine miles to Trenton through bitter cold, deep snow, and driving sleet.

When he attacked in the morning, his men found the Hessians (British-paid mercenary soldiers) asleep, often intoxicated, and poorly guarded. Washington's army killed about 40 soldiers and captured almost a thousand Hessians while about 400 escaped. The American army suffered only four deaths (two from freezing to death and two from wounds).

Washington immediately planned an attack on the British position at Princeton, New Jersey. He left a few men to tend campfires and to make noise while he secretly headed for Princeton, New Jersey. Leaving some of his troops to fight and delay the British near Trenton, on January 3, 1777, Washington's army forced the British forces at Princeton to surrender 200 men and lose another 100 casualties while the Americans suffered only 40 dead and wounded. These battles kept American morale alive through the winter and encouraged many soldiers to re-enlist for another year.

Revolutionary War Battles *(cont.)*

The Battle of Saratoga

In the summer of 1777, Howe skillfully defeated Washington's forces at Brandywine Creek, which allowed him to occupy Philadelphia. This forced the Continental Congress to establish temporary quarters in York, Pennsylvania. Washington tried to attack the British forces at Germantown and was forced to retreat again.

Meanwhile, General John Burgoyne was leading a British expedition south from Canada with the idea of hooking up with Howe's forces in New York City and cutting both the colony of New York and the new American nation in half. Burgoyne recaptured Fort Ticonderoga and then moved southward. American units ambushed his forces, destroyed bridges, cut off his supplies, and slowed his advance.

Hessians and Indians under Burgoyne's command were beaten at Bennington, Vermont, by newly mobilized companies of local militiamen. In mid-September 1777, Burgoyne was defeated by the Americans in a battle at Freeman's Farm, known as the first battle of Saratoga. In October he was beaten again in a second battle. As he began to retreat northward, Burgoyne was surrounded by American units and forced to surrender with his 6,000 men. The victory at Saratoga, New York, convinced the French that America could win the war, which helped them to eventually decide to become formal allies.

Valley Forge

American troops under Washington's command spent the winter of 1777–1778 camped at Valley Forge about 20 miles northwest of Philadelphia, Pennsylvania. Major military campaigns were usually not fought in the winter because weather conditions were so difficult. About 10,000 soldiers endured the harsh winter at Valley Forge. They suffered from severe cold, hunger, and illness. The Continental Congress was unable to provide a steady source of supplies, and the paper money printed by the government was virtually worthless because most citizens would not accept it. There was no gold in the national treasury to give it value.

Soldiers were forbidden to forage (gather or steal food from the surrounding farms), and they had no money to buy food or supplies. Their clothes were threadbare, torn, and filthy. Most of the men left bloody footprints in the snow because their shoes or boots were in shreds or gone entirely. Nonetheless, the men built log cabins to house themselves and made do with what they had. They trained with volunteer professional soldiers from Europe, especially Baron von Steuben and the Marquis de Lafayette.

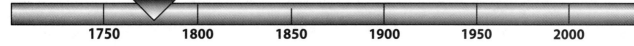
Revolutionary War Battles *(cont.)*

Vincennes and the West

Indians in the west attacked and destroyed American settlements and cooperated closely with their British allies. In 1778 George Rogers Clark led companies of frontier rangers to capture the British encampment at Kaskaskia. In the winter of 1779, he marched his small company of less than 200 men through the freezing, rugged wilderness to attack and defeat a much larger force of British and Indian allies encamped at a fort they had built in Vincennes at the juncture of the Ohio and Mississippi Rivers. The courage and determination of these few troops secured most of the west for the Americans, except for the British stronghold at Detroit.

Savannah, Charleston, and Camden

By 1778 the British had decided to concentrate their efforts in the south, get control of these colonies with the help of their Loyalist allies, and then move back north to finish off the American forces. In December 1778, British troops moved with speed and skill to capture Savannah, Georgia, and quickly advanced to control most of the state. In 1780 the British laid seige to Charleston, South Carolina, and in hard fighting forced the American commander to surrender his army of approximately 5,500 soldiers. This was the major American force in the south.

Local bands of militiamen quickly organized and harassed British troops throughout South Carolina. In July 1780, American forces clashed with those led by British General Cornwallis at Camden, South Carolina. The American forces were severely defeated, and it looked as if the end was near for the Americans.

King's Mountain, Cowpens, and Guilford Courthouse

Cornwallis decided to invade South Carolina and finish the job in the south. In October 1780, one entire division of his army was surrounded and captured by frontiersmen and local soldiers at King's Mountain. When American General Nathanael Greene took charge of the forces in the south, he divided his army into two commands and forced the British to pursue them. General Daniel Morgan, commanding a small force of superb riflemen and rangers, caught one British army at a cattle-grazing area called the Cowpens in South Carolina on January 17, 1781.

In a brilliant series of maneuvers, Morgan destroyed the British army led by the feared Colonel Banastre Tarleton. Greene and Morgan then battled British troops in March of 1781 at Guilford Courthouse in North Carolina, where they inflicted serious casualties on Cornwallis' army. The British were forced to regroup and no longer controlled the southern colonies.

Victory, Peace, and Aftermath

Victory at Yorktown

The British commander in America, Sir Henry Clinton, ordered General Cornwallis to move his troops into a defensive position along the coast of Virginia. It was clear that Clinton's southern strategy had not led to the control of Georgia and the Carolinas, and Clinton feared an attack on his forces in New York. Cornwallis moved to Yorktown, a town on a peninsula, where his troops could be loaded onto ships and sent to New York if needed.

In August 1781, Washington learned that French Admiral Francois de Grasse was taking his fleet of ships to Yorktown to bottle up Cornwallis and keep out British ships. French General Jean Baptiste Rochambeau with a force of 5,500 French soldiers and Washington with a force of about 12,000 troops moved south through Pennsylvania and Maryland to Virginia and surrounded Cornwallis.

De Grasse fought off an effort by a British fleet to rescue Cornwallis. French and American troops led by Washington along with militia from Virginia tightened the noose around the British forces. They set up a siege, attacking Cornwallis' fortifications with cannons and destroying any British units that left the stronghold. The British commander tried a desperate effort to ferry his men in rafts and small boats across the York River to escape the trap. Stormy weather prevented the crossing, however, and on October 19, 1781, Cornwallis surrendered his 8,000-man army—about one-fourth of all British troops in America.

Treaty of Paris

The war didn't actually end with the surrender at Yorktown, but the British realized it was over. Fighting continued in small skirmishes and minor battles for almost two years, but the defeat of Cornwallis led to a change of leadership in London. The new leaders insisted that Parliament and the king make peace. Discussions began in April 1782 in Paris. Benjamin Franklin, John Adams, and John Jay were the primary negotiators for the United States. These discussions were contentious. The British government knew they had to make peace and accept the existence of the United States as an independent nation, but they were reluctant to loosen their long-held control of the colonies. The final, formal Treaty of Paris was signed on September 3, 1783.

Victory, Peace, and Aftermath *(cont.)*

The Terms of Peace

The terms of peace were actually quite generous. The British retained control of Canada, but they relinquished control of the 13 colonies and all the land they claimed from Canada to Spanish Florida and from the Atlantic coast to the Mississippi River. This included the Indian lands in the Ohio and Mississippi River valleys that they had forbidden American pioneers to settle in. The British agreed to remove their troops from American territory.

The Loyalists, or Tories, who had supported Britain were promised that their confiscated land and property would be returned or paid for by the American government, but that was rarely done. Thousands of Loyalists departed for England on British ships or moved to Canada to escape the anger of the newly liberated colonists.

Costs of the War

The new nation was bankrupt and owed huge war debts to France, Spain, and other countries. These debts would finally be paid after a new government was created with the power to tax. Over 7,000 Americans were killed in battle, and at least 8,000 more were wounded. More than 10,000 died from disease, hunger, and exposure to the elements. In addition, more than 8,500 American soldiers died in British prisons from brutal mistreatment, starvation, and disease. More than 1,000 American soldiers were missing and never accounted for. The British lost about 10,000 dead from the war.

A New Form of Government

The American states had won their liberty from British colonial rule. Now they had to make the new nation work. The first few years after the war were troubled. Under the Articles of Confederation, the government was very weak and did not have the power to enforce decisions on individual states, collect taxes, pay debts, or maintain an army for the protection of the nation.

In 1787 representatives from 12 of the states met in Philadelphia to form a more effective government. They discarded the weak Articles of Confederation and created a government which allowed states to retain much of their independence but required them to work together to support a national government having real power. Under the newly adopted Constitution of the United States, this government could enforce laws and treaties, collect taxes for the common defense of the states, and provide a framework for a successful nation.

The American Colonies Before the Revolution Quiz

Directions: Read pages 8 and 9 about the American colonies before the Revolution. Answer the questions below by circling the correct answer. Then underline the sentence in the article where the answer is found.

1. In which colony were the first English settlements in New England located?
   a. Connecticut
   b. Rhode Island
   c. Virginia
   d. Massachusetts

2. Which religious group founded Plymouth Colony and the Massachusetts Bay Colony?
   a. Puritans
   b. Church of England
   c. Catholics
   d. Quakers

3. William Penn intended his colony to be a haven for Quakers. What does *haven* mean?
   a. farm land
   b. church
   c. place of safety
   d. seaport

4. Which was the largest city in the New England colonies?
   a. New York
   b. Boston
   c. Philadelphia
   d. Baltimore

5. In which colony was the first permanent English settlement in North America located?
   a. Massachusetts
   b. Pennsylvania
   c. Virginia
   d. Maryland

6. Georgia was founded as a refuge for which group of people?
   a. Quakers
   b. debtors
   c. Puritans
   d. Catholics

7. In which year did Carolina split into two colonies?
   a. 1607
   b. 1729
   c. 1620
   d. 1663

8. Which plant produces a blue dye?
   a. indigo
   b. tobacco
   c. wheat
   d. rice

9. Which colony was renamed New York?
   a. New Jersey
   b. New Sweden
   c. New Netherland
   d. New England

10. Which group of colonies grew cash crops on plantations and used black slaves for farming?
    a. Southern
    b. Middle Atlantic
    c. New England
    d. New York

The Causes of the War Quiz

Directions: Read pages 10–13 about the causes of the American Revolution. Answer the questions below by circling the correct answer. Then underline the sentence in the article where the answer is found.

1. The Seven Years' War was fought between Britain and which world power?
   a. Germany
   b. France
   c. America
   d. Canada

2. Which British law placed a tax on newspapers and playing cards?
   a. Townshend Acts
   b. Sugar Act
   c. Stamp Act
   d. Intolerable Acts

3. How many rioters were killed in the Boston Massacre?
   a. 35
   b. several thousands
   c. 5
   d. none

4. Who was the commander of the British forces in Boston?
   a. George Grenville
   b. Paul Revere
   c. Samuel Adams
   d. General Gage

5. In which city did the first battle of the American Revolution occur?
   a. Boston
   b. Concord
   c. Lexington
   d. Philadelphia

6. Which laws were passed by the British authorities to punish the city of Boston for the Boston Tea Party?
   a. Stamp Act
   b. Townshend Acts
   c. Intolerable Acts
   d. Proclamation of 1763

7. Why did the British forbid the American colonists to settle in the Ohio River Valley?
   a. to avoid war with Indians
   b. to collect taxes easier
   c. to stop tea smuggling
   d. because it belonged to France

8. Who led the Sons of Liberty and organized the Committees of Correspondence?
   a. John Adams
   b. John Hancock
   c. Paul Revere
   d. Samuel Adams

9. What does the word *correspondence* mean?
   a. paying taxes
   b. writing letters
   c. tea parties
   d. rioting

10. What does the word *boycott* mean?
    a. collecting taxes
    b. refusing to buy goods
    c. selling goods
    d. smuggling

American Revolutionary Leaders Quiz

Directions: Read pages 14–16 about the men who led the American Revolution. Answer the questions below by circling the correct answer. Then underline the sentence in the article where the answer is found.

1. Who served as Pennsylvania's agent in London from 1757 to 1775?
   a. Samuel Adams
   b. Ben Franklin
   c. Thomas Jefferson
   d. John Hancock

2. Who was the principal author of the Declaration of Independence?
   a. Thomas Jefferson
   b. Ben Franklin
   c. John Adams
   d. Samuel Adams

3. Who is called the "Father of the American Revolution"?
   a. John Adams
   b. John Hancock
   c. Samuel Adams
   d. Patrick Henry

4. Who wrote *The Letters from a Farmer in Pennsylvania*?
   a. John Hancock
   b. John Dickinson
   c. John Adams
   d. Paul Revere

5. Who rode out of Boston to warn Adams and Hancock that British soldiers were coming?
   a. Paul Revere
   b. Patrick Henry
   c. Thomas Jefferson
   d. John Adams

6. Who was the first signer of the Declaration of Independence?
   a. Thomas Jefferson
   b. Benjamin Franklin
   c. John Hancock
   d. Patrick Henry

7. Who gave a speech in which he said, "Give me liberty or give me death"?
   a. Patrick Henry
   b. Thomas Jefferson
   c. Samuel Adams
   d. Paul Revere

8. Who died on the fiftieth anniversary of the Declaration of Independence?
   a. Samuel Adams
   b. Thomas Jefferson
   c. John Hancock
   d. Benjamin Franklin

9. Who nominated George Washington as commander of the American army?
   a. Samuel Adams
   b. Thomas Jefferson
   c. John Adams
   d. John Dickinson

10. John Adams was a powerful orator. What does *orator* mean?
    a. writer
    b. leader
    c. legislator
    d. public speaker

Revolutionary Soldiers Quiz

Directions: Read pages 17–19 about the soldiers of the American Revolution. Answer the questions below by circling the correct answer. Then underline the sentence in the article where the answer is found.

1. Who disguised herself as a man and fought in the Continental army?
   a. Mary Hays
   b. Deborah Sampson
   c. Margaret Corbin
   d. Marquis de Lafayette

2. Which American officer controlled most of the western frontier during the war?
   a. "Mad" Anthony Wayne
   b. George Washington
   c. George Rogers Clark
   d. Nathanael Greene

3. Who is known as the "Father of His Country"?
   a. George Washington
   b. Thomas Jefferson
   c. Alexander Hamilton
   d. Nathan Hale

4. Who was the schoolteacher hanged by the British as an American spy?
   a. Anthony Wayne
   b. Nathan Hale
   c. Henry Lee
   d. Margaret Corbin

5. Who was the greatest American cavalry leader of the war?
   a. Henry Lee
   b. Anthony Wayne
   c. Marquis de Lafayette
   d. Nathanael Greene

6. How do the soldiers in the cavalry fight?
   a. on horseback
   b. in airplanes
   c. on ships
   d. on foot

7. Who served as a personal aide to General Washington?
   a. Henry Lee
   b. Alexander Hamilton
   c. Nathan Hale
   d. George Rogers Clark

8. Who came to America from France at the age of 19 to fight in the war?
   a. Nathan Hale
   b. Henry Lee
   c. Marquis de Lafayette
   d. Alexander Hamilton

9. Who was the youngest brigadier general in the American army and later quartermaster general?
   a. Nathanael Greene
   b. Henry Lee
   c. Alexander Hamilton
   d. Anthony Wayne

10. Who ordered his small force of men to attack the entire army of General Cornwallis?
    a. "Light-Horse Harry" Lee
    b. "Mad" Anthony Wayne
    c. "Captain Molly" Corbin
    d. George Rogers Clark

The Declaration of Independence Quiz

Directions: Read pages 20 and 21 about the Declaration of Independence. Answer the questions below by circling the correct answer. Then underline the sentence in the article where the answer is found.

1. Who introduced a resolution in the Continental Congress calling for independence from Great Britain?
   a. George Washington
   b. John Hancock
   c. Thomas Jefferson
   d. Richard Henry Lee

2. Which member of the committee was chosen to write the Declaration of Independence characterized himself as "obnoxious, suspected, and unpopular"?
   a. John Adams
   b. Thomas Jefferson
   c. John Hancock
   d. Benjamin Franklin

3. How many changes in Jefferson's draft of the Declaration did Congress make?
   a. none
   b. 2
   c. about 80
   d. about 12

4. How long did Jefferson take to write the draft of the Declaration?
   a. 4 years
   b. 2 days
   c. 2 months
   d. 2½ weeks

5. How many members of Congress signed the Declaration of Independence?
   a. 300
   b. 56
   c. 80
   d. none

6. Who wrote his signature in a large script so that King George could read it without his spectacles?
   a. Thomas Jefferson
   b. George Washington
   c. Benjamin Franklin
   d. John Hancock

7. What are militias?
   a. writers
   b. public speakers
   c. citizen soldiers
   d. legislators

8. What would southern representatives in the Continental Congress not accept as part of the Declaration?
   a. the idea of natural rights
   b. separation from Great Britain
   c. an end to slavery
   d. taxes on tobacco

9. Which colony did Roger Sherman represent on the Committee of Five?
   a. Connecticut
   b. Rhode Island
   c. Pennsylvania
   d. Virginia

10. What were the signers of the Declaration prepared to pledge?
    a. their children
    b. their futures
    c. their sacred honor
    d. their land

Revolutionary War Battles Quiz

Directions: Read pages 22–25 about the battles of the American Revolution. Answer the questions below by circling the correct answer. Then underline the sentence in the article where the answer is found.

1. Which was the deadliest single battle of the American Revolution?
   a. Trenton
   b. Breed's Hill (Bunker Hill)
   c. Saratoga
   d. Battle of Long Island

2. Who commanded the British forces at Bunker Hill?
   a. General Clinton
   b. General Cornwallis
   c. General Gage
   d. Colonel Tarleton

3. What battle occurred the day after Christmas in 1776?
   a. Princeton
   b. Long Island
   c. Bunker Hill
   d. Trenton

4. Who led the rangers who captured Vincennes?
   a. George Rogers Clark
   b. George Washington
   c. General Cornwallis
   d. General Morgan

5. What word means "to gather or steal food"?
   a. regroup
   b. forage
   c. harass
   d. evacuate

6. Who led Americans to victory at the battle of Cowpens?
   a. George Rogers Clark
   b. Ethan Allen
   c. Nathanael Green
   d. Dan Morgan

7. Which word means "dead and wounded soldiers"?
   a. casualties
   b. evacuate
   c. militia
   d. allies

8. Which victory was important because it convinced the French to make a formal alliance with the United States?
   a. Bunker Hill
   b. Long Island
   c. Trenton
   d. Saratoga

9. Henry Knox was an artillery officer. Which weapons did his men use?
   a. muskets
   b. cannons
   c. rifles
   d. sabers

10. Which word refers to "British-paid mercenary soldiers"?
    a. rangers
    b. Hessians
    c. Loyalists
    d. Tories

Victory, Peace, and Aftermath Quiz

Directions: Read pages 26 and 27 about the victory, peace, and aftermath of the war. Answer the questions below by circling the correct answer in each question below. Underline the sentence in the article where the answer is found.

1. Who was the commander of the British forces in America?
   a. General Washington
   b. General Cornwallis
   c. Sir Henry Clinton
   d. Admiral De Grasse

2. Which man did not help negotiate the Treaty of Paris for the Americans?
   a. Benjamin Franklin
   b. George Washington
   c. John Jay
   d. John Adams

3. How many men did General Cornwallis surrender at Yorktown?
   a. 8,000
   b. 5,500
   c. 12,000
   d. 10,000

4. How many American prisoners died in British prisons during the war?
   a. 7,000
   b. 10,000
   c. 8,500
   d. 1,000

5. Why did the representatives in Philadelphia create the Constitution of the United States?
   a. to make a stronger nation
   b. to enforce laws and treaties
   c. to attack the British
   d. Both A and B

6. Who fought off a British fleet trying to rescue General Cornwallis?
   a. General Rochambeau
   b. Admiral de Grasse
   c. General Washington
   d. Sir Henry Clinton

7. Where is Yorktown located?
   a. New York
   b. Georgia
   c. Virginia
   d. Maryland

8. Which French commander brought troops to help Washington surround Cornwallis' army?
   a. General Rochambeau
   b. Admiral de Grasse
   c. Sir Henry Clinton
   d. John Adams

9. What document was signed on September 3, 1783?
   a. Articles of Confederation
   b. Constitution of the U.S.
   c. Treaty of Paris
   d. Declaration of Independence

10. After the war, what did many of the Loyalists in America do?
   a. They moved to Canada.
   b. They went to Paris.
   c. They moved to England.
   d. Both A and C

Teacher Lesson Plans for Language Arts

Vocabulary, Spelling, Almanacs, and Proverbs

Objectives: Students will learn to apply their language arts skills in vocabulary and spelling. Students will learn to use almanacs. Students will recognize and understand proverbs.

Materials: copies of The Lexicon of Liberty (page 37); copies of Spelling Then and Now (page 38); copies of *Poor Richard's Almanack* (page 39); copies of Proverbs and Aphorisms (page 40)

Procedure

1. Reproduce and distribute The Lexicon of Liberty (page 37) activity sheet. Review the vocabulary and pronunciation if necessary. Have students do the assigned page.

2. Reproduce and distribute the Spelling Then and Now (page 38) activity sheet. Review the changes in spelling styles. Have students study the word list with a partner before each student writes sentences using the words correctly.

3. Reproduce and distribute the *Poor Richard's Almanack* (page 39) activity sheet. Review the types of material that Franklin included in his almanac. Have your students consult an almanac and complete the page with facts usually found in modern almanacs.

4. Reproduce and distribute the Proverbs and Aphorisms (page 40) activity sheet. Explain that proverbs and aphorisms usually express an obvious truth. Help students translate the meaning of the proverbs into their own words. Allow students to finish the page and then review the meanings together.

Assessment: Have students share information derived from almanacs with the class. Have students share the meanings of proverbs and their rewritten versions with the class.

Poetry and Literature

Objectives: Students will develop skills in reading and understanding poetry. Students will read from and respond to a variety of fictional accounts of the American Revolution.

Materials: copies of *Paul Revere's Ride* (pages 41–43); copies of Figurative Language in *Paul Revere's Ride* (page 44); copies of Narrative Poetry in Two Voices (page 45); copies of Diaries (page 46); copies of *Common Sense* (page 47); copies of *Sarah Bishop* (page 48); copies of *Why Don't You Get a Horse, Sam Adams?* and *And Then What Happened, Paul Revere?* (page 49); copies of Focus on Author Jean Fritz (pages 50 and 51); literature selections mentioned in this section including *Sarah Bishop*, *The Winter of Red Snow: The Revolutionary War Diary of Abigail Jane Stewart*, and *My Brother Sam Is Dead*; copies of the poems listed on page 45

Procedure

1. Reproduce and distribute the *Paul Revere's Ride* (pages 41–43) activity sheets. Review the nature of poetry in two voices and stress the importance of timing so that the two voices work in unison. You may want to assign this activity to one or several pairs of capable students and use the presentations as an example for doing the narrative poems on page 45. Have students review the vocabulary and figurative language on pages 43 and 44 to increase comprehension and understanding.

Teacher Lesson Plans for Language Arts

Poetry and Literature *(cont.)*

Procedure *(cont.)*

2. Reproduce and distribute the Narrative Poetry in Two Voices (page 45) activity sheet. Review the techniques for reciting poetry with a partner. Assign poems from page 45 to each team of students. Remind students to divide the poem and choose several sections to do as a chorus. Have students practice their poems for several days before presenting to the class.

3. Reproduce and distribute the Diaries (page 46) activity sheet. Have students read the book and complete the comprehension questions.

4. Reproduce and distribute the *Common Sense* (page 47) activity sheet. Explain the idea of bias and distortion in news reporting. Have students read and analyze the articles as outlined on the page.

5. Reproduce and distribute the *Sarah Bishop* (page 48) activity sheet. Assign the book to an individual, a group, or the class, depending on your supply of books. Have students complete the comprehension questions and the creative writing activity. Encourage students to read *My Brother Sam Is Dead* as an extension activity.

6. Reproduce and distribute the *Why Don't You Get a Horse, Sam Adams?* and *And Then What Happened, Paul Revere?* (page 49) and Focus on Author Jean Fritz (pages 50 and 51) activity pages. Have students complete the comprehension questions, read about Jean Fritz, and select another of her books to read.

7. Reproduce and distribute The Language of the Declaration of Independence (page 52), the Readers' Theater Notes (page 53), and the Readers' Theater Script: The Declaration of Independence (pages 54–56). Review the vocabulary of the Declaration of Independence on page 52. Have students practice and then perform the readers' theater script.

Assessment: Have students present to the entire class. Base performance assessments on pacing, volume, expression, and focus of the participants. Use student activity pages and class discussions to assess students' performance on the literature selections.

The Lexicon of Liberty

Directions: Match each word in Column 1 with its correct meaning in Column 2. Use a dictionary, glossary, and student-reading pages to help define these words related to the birth of the United States.

Column 1	Column 2
1. *revolution*	a. to sneak something into a country illegally
2. *democracy*	b. people who have a legal right to live in a country
3. *smuggle*	c. to refuse to buy goods
4. *tax*	d. elected representatives who make laws
5. *patriot*	e. to lawfully oppose a government
6. *boycott*	f. government by the people
7. *Congress*	g. a person who stirs people to action
8. *correspondence*	h. money collected by a government
9. *stockpile*	i. a person who loves his country
10. *citizens*	j. the overthrow of a government
11. *declaration*	k. Britain's elected legislature
12. *intolerable*	l. written letters
13. *treason*	m. a statement of intentions
14. *protest*	n. unbearable; impossible to accept
15. *independent*	o. free of control by another
16. *Loyalist*	p. a mass killing of many people
17. *propaganda*	q. to betray your country
18. *massacre*	r. stored up goods or weapons
19. *Parliament*	s. a colonist who supported England
20. *agitator*	t. promoting ideas in books, papers, or pictures

Spelling Then and Now

*"When in the course of human events, it becomes **necefsary** for one people to **difsolve** the political bands which have connected them with another, and to **afsume** among the powers of the earth, the **feparate** and equal **ftation** . . ."*

*"Plain and **eafy** Means for **Perfons** to cure **themfelves** of all, or **moft** of the **Diftempers**, incident to this Climate . . ."*

*"A farmer will take out the plough when the **colour** of the earth is dark brown . . ."*

*"Her **favourite** interest was **musick** not **mathematicks** . . ."*

In the era of the American Revolution, a variety of spellings were used for some words. In some words, an "f" was often used for "s." The words *color* and *flavor* were spelled "colour" and "flavour." Words ending in "ic" often ended in "ick." Noah Webster, an American soldier during the Revolution, spent most of his lifetime creating a standard, simplified method of spelling and writing dictionaries of the American language.

Assignment

1. Rewrite each of the above quotations using today's spelling for the words in boldface.

2. Write sentences using 10 of the following words correctly.

Words Often Misspelled

accept (agree to)	**environment**	**receive**
believe	**except** (leave out)	**their** (belonging to them)
chief	**feisty**	**themselves**
collected	**friend**	**there** (place)
colossal	**frontier**	**they're** (they are)
committee	**government**	**wear** (put on clothes)
competent	**harass**	**weigh**
deaf (can't hear)	**heir**	**where**
death (not alive)	**hole** (an empty place)	**which** (what one)
deceive	**language**	**while**
decided	**lying**	**whole** (all)
different	**necessary**	**witch** (the woman)
dying	**neighbor**	**you're** (you are)
enemy	**occurrence**	**your** (belongs to you)

Poor Richard's Almanack

Poor Richard's Almanack was published annually by Benjamin Franklin for 26 years, starting in 1732. It was immensely popular and contained a wide variety of facts, sayings, weather predictions, astronomical information, historical dates, and many similar pieces of information. Below are some examples.

Maxims

"Well done, is twice done."

"If you would keep your Secret from an enemy, tell it not to a friend."

Useful Information

"How to make a Striking Sundial"

"The great Blazing-star or Comet . . .will appear again in 1757"

"How to Secure Houses . . . from LIGHTNING"

Advice

"HINTS for those that would be Rich"

"Rules of Health and long Life"

Assignment

Today almanacs are usually published yearly. They have a wide variety of information on history, geography, science, entertainment, sports, and government. They rarely offer advice, and few efforts are made to be amusing or clever. Use an almanac to find the following information.

1. List two events from the year _____ .

    a. _____   b. _____

2. List two states and at least one fact about each state.

    a. _____

    b. _____

3. List two science facts.

    a. _____   b. _____

4. List two sports facts.

    a. _____   b. _____

Proverbs and Aphorisms

Proverbs and aphorisms are short popular sayings that express a truth which seems obvious. Benjamin Franklin often rephrased or updated popular proverbs of his time.

Assignment

Read each proverb below. Then paraphrase this proverb, rewriting it in your own words. The first two are done for you.

1. "Still waters run deep."

   Quiet people often have important ideas to share.

2. "Money is a good servant, but a bad master."

   Don't let money control your life.

3. "A watched pot never boils."

   _____

4. "A good example is the best sermon."

   _____

5. "Truth is stranger than fiction."

   _____

6. "He who lives by the sword, will die by the sword."

   _____

7. "It's easier to prevent bad habits than to break them."

   _____

8. "Time and tide wait for no man."

   _____

9. "Necessity is the mother of invention."

   _____

10. "Never put off till tomorrow what may be done today."

    _____

11. "Beauty is only skin deep."

    _____

12. "The coward dies a thousand deaths; the brave man dies but once."

    _____

Paul Revere's Ride

Paul Revere's Ride is a poem that is arranged to be read by two readers with the chorus being read together. Read the poem silently several times, and check the meanings of the words in the vocabulary section at the end of the poem. Decide who will be the first and second reader. Practice reading the poem together several times. Then present your reading to the class.

First Speaker

Paul Revere's Ride
by Henry Wadsworth Longfellow

Chorus

Listen, my children, and you shall hear
Of the midnight ride of Paul Revere,
On the eighteenth of April, in Seventy-five;
Hardly a man is now alive
Who remembers that famous day and year.

First Speaker

He said to his friend, "If the British march
By land or sea from the town tonight,
Hang a lantern aloft in the belfry arch
Of the North Church tower as a signal light –

Chorus

One, if by land, and two, if by sea;
And I on the opposite shore will be,
Ready to ride and spread the alarm
Through every Middlesex village and farm,
For the country folk to be up and to arm."

Second Speaker

Then he said "Good-night," and with muffled oar
Silently row'd to the Charlestown shore,
Just as the moon rose over the bay,
Where swinging wide at her moorings lay
The Somerset, British man-of-war;

Chorus

A phantom ship, with each mast and spar
Across the moon like a prison bar,
And a huge black hulk, that was magnified
By its own reflection in the tide.

First Speaker

Meanwhile his friend, through alley and street,
Wanders and watches with eager ears,
Till in the silence around him he hears
The master of men at the barrack-door,
The sound of arms, and the tramp of feet,
And the measured tread of the grenadiers
Marching down to their boats on the shore.

Second Speaker

Then he climb'd the tower of the Old North
    Church,
By the wooden stairs, with stealthy tread,
To the belfry-chamber overhead,
And startled the pigeons from their perch
On the sombre rafters, that round him made
Masses of moving shapes of shade –

First Speaker

By the trembling ladder, steep and tall,
To the highest window in the wall,
Where he paused to listen and look down
A moment on the roofs of the town,
And the moonlight flowing over all.

Chorus

Beneath, in the churchyard, lay the dead,
In their night-encampment on the hill,
Wrapp'd in silence so deep and still
That he could hear, like a sentinel's tread,
The watchful night-wind, as it went
Creeping along from tent to tent,
And seeming to whisper, "All is well!"

Paul Revere's Ride *(cont.)*

First Speaker

A moment only he feels the spell
Of the place and the hour, and the secret dread
Of the lonely belfry and the dead;
For suddenly all his thoughts are bent
On a shadowy something far away,
Where the river widens to meet the bay,
A line of black that bends and floats
On the rising tide like a bridge of boats.

Second Speaker

Meanwhile, impatient to mount and ride,
Booted and spurr'd, with a heavy stride
On the opposite shore walk'd Paul Revere.
Now he patted his horse's side,
Now he gazed at the landscape far and near,
Then, impetuous, stamp'd the earth,
And turn'd and tighten'd his saddle-girth;
But mostly he watch'd with eager search

First Speaker

The belfry-tower of the Old North Church,
As it rose above the graves on the hill,
Lonely and spectral and sombre and still.
And lo! as he looks, on the belfry's height
A glimmer, and then a gleam of light!
He springs to the saddle, the bridle he turns,
But lingers and gazes, till full on his sight
A second lamp in the belfry burns.

Chorus

A hurry of hoofs in a village street,
A shape in the moonlight, a bulk in the dark,
And beneath, from the pebbles, in passing, a spark
Struck out by a steed flying fearless and fleet:
That was all; and yet, through the gloom and the
  light,
The fate of a nation was riding that night;
And the spark struck out by that steed in his flight
Kindled the land into flame with its heat.

Second Speaker

He had left the village and mounted the steep,
And beneath him, tranquil and broad and deep,
Is the Mystic, meeting the ocean tides,
And under the alders that skirt its edge,
Now soft on the sand, now loud on the ledge,
Is heard the tramp of his steed as he rides.

First Speaker

It was twelve by the village clock
When he crossed the bridge into Medford town.
He heard the crowing of the cock,
And the barking of the farmer's dog,
And felt the damp of the river fog,
That rises after the sun goes down.

Second Speaker

It was one by the village clock
When he galloped into Lexington.
He saw the gilded weathercock
Swim in the moonlight as he pass'd,

Chorus

And the meeting-house windows, blank and bare,
Gaze at him with a spectral glare,
As if they already stood aghast
At the bloody work they would look upon.

Second Speaker

It was two by the village clock
When he came to the bridge in Concord town.
He heard the bleating of the flock,
And the twitter of birds among the trees,
And felt the breath of the morning breeze
Blowing over the meadows brown.

First Speaker

And one was safe and asleep in his bed
Who at the bridge would be first to fall,
Who that day would be lying dead,
Pierced by a British musket-ball.

Paul Revere's Ride (cont.)

Second Speaker

You know the rest; in the books you have read,
How the British regulars fired and fled,
How the farmers gave them ball for ball,
From behind each fence and farmyard wall,
Chasing the red-coats down the lane,
Then crossing the fields to emerge again
Under the trees at the turn of the road,
And only pausing to fire and load.

First Speaker

So through the night rode Paul Revere,
And so through the night went his cry of alarm
To every Middlesex village and farm –

Chorus

A cry of defiance, and not of fear,
A voice in the darkness, a knock at the door,
And a word that shall echo for evermore!

Second Speaker

For, borne on the night-wind of the Past,
Through all our history, to the last,
In the hour of darkness, and peril, and need,

Chorus

The people will waken and listen to hear
The hurrying hoof-beats of that steed,
And the midnight message of Paul Revere.

Vocabulary

aghast—horrified

alders—birch trees

barrack—soldier's living quarters

belfry—bell tower

bleating—sheep sounds

booted and spurr'd—wearing boots and spurs

bridle—head harness to guide a horse

defiance—bold resistance

emerge—to come out of

fleet—fast

grenadiers—elite troops

impetuous—anxious to get started

man-of-war—warship

mast and spar—poles to hold sails

mooring—cables holding a ship

musket-ball—bullet

Mystic—a river near Boston

night-encampment—soldiers' night camp

peril—danger

phantom—ghost

red-coats—British soldiers

sentinel's tread—a sentry's walk

sombre—dark and gloomy

spectral glare—ghostly stare

spectral—ghost-like

steed—powerful horse

tranquil—peaceful

weathercock—weathervane

Figurative Language in *Paul Revere's Ride*

Poets use *figurative language* to paint word pictures for the reader and the listener. Personification, simile, and metaphor are three types of figurative language.

Personification

Personification is a technique used to make something that is not human feel or act like a person.

> "The watchful night-wind, as it went
> Creeping along from tent to tent,"

The wind at night is compared to a person sneaking along from one tent to another.

Metaphor

A *metaphor* is a comparison where one thing is spoken of as if it was another.

> "Beneath, in the churchyard, lay the dead,
> In their night-encampment on the hill,"

The dead are compared to soldiers in camp for the night.

Simile

A *simile* is a comparison of two different things using *like* or *as*.

> "A phantom ship, with each mast and spar
> Across the moon like a prison bar,"

The mast of the ship is compared to the bars of a prison.

Rhyme

Poets use rhyming words at the end of lines of poetry to achieve a pleasing effect and to highlight some aspect of the poem, such as the "marching" and "riding" in *Paul Revere's Ride*.

Assignment

1. Find and discuss these examples of personification in the poem *Paul Revere's Ride*.
   a. "And felt the breath . . ."
   b. "He saw the gilded . . ."
   c. "And the meeting-house . . ."

2. Find and discuss these samples of metaphor in the poem.
   a. "A line of black . . ."
   b. "On the sombre rafters . . ."

3. Find and discuss these samples of simile in the poem.
   a. "... like a sentinel's . . ."
   b. "As if they already stood aghast . . ."
   c. " . . . like a bridge . . ."

4. List the last words of each line in the poem. What pattern did you find?

5. Does every ending word have a rhyming partner in another line?

Narrative Poetry in Two Voices

Reading poetry aloud with a friend is a special way to enjoy poetry. In this type of presentation, two or more students recite a poem together, reciting alternate verses or stanzas throughout the poem and reading some sections together as a choral reading. Use *Paul Revere's Ride* on the previous pages as an example for dividing your own poem.

This technique can be used with any poem but it is especially effective with ballads and story poems like *Paul Revere's Ride*, *Annabel Lee*, and *The Charge of the Light Brigade*. For poems written to be read in two voices, use Paul Fleishman's Newbery Award-winning *Joyful Noise*, a collection of poems about insects.

Assignment

With a partner, select a poem from the list below or one that your teacher has provided or approved. Choose a poem that appeals to you because of the rhyme, rhythm, or subject matter. Divide the poem into parts so that you and your partner can recite the poem back and forth together. Choose at least a few lines that both of you will recite aloud together and do the following.

1. Copy your poem so that each of you has a copy to work with.

2. Practice together so that you have the same speed, volume, and pace.

3. Underline words which should receive special emphasis and try to get a feel for the force and flow of the poetic language.

4. Practice several times over the course of a week or more.

5. Recite the poem for the class.

Suggested Poems

An Old-Time Sea Fight. Walt Whitman.
Annabel Lee. Edgar Allan Poe.
The Ballad of the Oysterman. Oliver Wendell Holmes.
Barbara Frietchie. John Greenleaf Whittier.
The Bells. Edgar Allan Poe.
Casey at the Bat. Ernest Lawrence Thayer.
Casey Jones. Anonymous.
The Charge of the Light Brigade. Lord Alfred Tennyson.
The Cremation of Sam McGee. Robert W. Service.
The Death of King Arthur. Lord Alfred Tennyson.
Eldorado. Edgar Allan Poe.
Epitaph for a Concord Boy. Stanley Young.
The Highwayman. Alfred Noyes.
John Henry. Anonymous.
Lochinvar. Sir Walter Scott.
Lord Randall. Anonymous.
Ode to Billy Joe. Bobbie Gentry.
The Skeleton in Armor. Henry Wadsworth Longfellow.
The Walrus and the Carpenter. Lewis Carroll.

Diaries

The Winter of Red Snow: The Revolutionary War Diary of Abigail Jane Stewart by Kristiana Gregory (Scholastic, 1996) is a fictional, first-person account of the winter at Valley Forge as seen through the eyes of a young girl. Abigail's family lives near Valley Forge, and her mother does laundry for General Washington and his wife Martha when she comes to spend the winter.

The book portrays intimate details of everyday life, and the reader gets a real sense of the hardships endured both by the soldiers and those who try to help them. Abigail watches a soldier's leg being amputated because severe cold has caused gangrene. She sees a woman whipped for treason and soldiers drummed out of the army for desertion. She shares General Washington's birthday cake and watches Baron von Steuben drilling the soldiers.

Assignment

Read *The Winter of Red Snow: The Revolutionary War Diary of Abigail Jane Stewart*. Then answer the following questions on a separate sheet of paper. Afterwards, discuss the book with other students.

1. Why did Lucy have her hair cut?

2. How did her parents punish Lucy?

3. How did the five Fitzgerald boys die at the same time?

4. Why did the soldiers steal from the neighbors?

5. What was Papa's occupation?

6. How did the Quakers feel about the war? Why?

7. Who was Sir Billy?

8. Why did some Americans sell food and supplies to the British?

9. How did Baron von Steuben communicate with the soldiers?

10. Who bought the wig made from Lucy's hair?

Extension

1. In Revolutionary times, many people kept diaries to record the events of their lives and their deepest feelings. Start a diary of your own and make entries every day for two weeks. Record the simple things that happen in your daily life, the important things that occur in the world, and your feelings.

2. Read *Mary Alice Peale: Philadelphia, 1777* (Aladdin, 1996). The heroine of this story is caught between two loyalties. Her family has remained loyal to the British and even hosted British officers in their home. However, her brother William has joined the American army to fight against British rule. While a grand party is going on in their Philadelphia home, William is hiding in their garden shed, severely wounded.

Common Sense

Thomas Paine was an immigrant from England who arrived in Philadelphia in 1774 ready to start a new life. He quickly got caught up in the flow of events leading to independence from Britain. In 1776 he published his pamphlet *Common Sense*. It was written in a simple, direct style that was easily read by the common people. The basic theme of the pamphlet was clear: the people should rule. As evidenced in the excerpt below, Paine used dramatic language, exaggeration, and "good-versus-evil" comparisons to convince his readers to support independence.

"O! ye that love mankind! Ye that dare oppose not only tyranny but the tyrant, stand forth! . . . These are the times that try men's souls. The summer soldier and the sunshine patriot will, in this crisis, shrink from the service of their country; but he that stands it now, deserves the love and thanks of man and woman. Tyranny, like Hell, is not easily conquered . . ."

Most authors of books, magazine articles, and newspaper stories have a clear set of beliefs which underline what they write. Writers use their skills to convince readers about the message they are trying to convey. Even factual articles that appear fair and balanced are often slanted toward a specific opinion on an issue.

Assignment

Read three articles on any subject of current public interest found in magazines, newspapers, or Internet Web sites. The subject can deal with politics, health care, education, the environment, childcare, crime and punishment, war, immigration, or any similar topic. Then select one of the articles, and complete the following outline.

1. Title of the article: _____

2. Subject of the article: _____

3. The writer's opinion about the issue: _____

   _____

4. Words or phrases the author used to praise or support one person or idea: _____

   _____

5. Words or phrases the author used to demean or oppose a person or idea: _____

   _____

6. List three facts expressed in the article.

   a. _____

   b. _____

   c. _____

7. List three opinions expressed in the article.

   a. _____

   b. _____

   c. _____

| 1750 | 1800 | 1850 | 1900 | 1950 | 2000 |

Sarah Bishop

The war for American independence created fierce conflicts in most of the communities where Americans lived. Like many colonial families, Sarah Bishop's family was torn apart by divided loyalties. Her father supported the British and was very vocal in support of the king and his troops. Her brother Chad went off to war on the patriots' side without her father's blessing. Sarah's father is killed by rampaging supporters of independence, and her brother is captured by the British and jailed on a British prison ship where he endures starvation, disease, and the savagery of his captors.

Sarah is a 15-year-old orphan without family or friends who is caught in the crossfire of divided loyalties, personal hatreds, and ruthless warfare raging throughout the northern colonies. Sarah's intelligence, determination, courage, and resolve are tested as she tries to find her brother and to survive alone in the wilderness. She is treated as an outcast, a witch, and a traitor, but she does not surrender her spirit.

Assignment

Read *Sarah Bishop* by Scott O'Dell. Then answer the following questions on a separate sheet of paper.

1. Who killed Sarah's father? Why?

2. What happened to Sarah's brother Chad?

3. Why was Sarah accused of being a witch?

4. Why was Colonel Cunningham searching for Sarah?

5. Who helped Sarah learn to survive in the wilderness?

6. Who was Sam Goshen and why was Sarah afraid of him?

7. Why was Sarah put in jail by Constable Hawkins?

8. Write a short paragraph stating your opinion about one of the following questions. Give your reasons, based on what you know about the American Revolution and the events that occurred in the story.

   • Which side would you have supported in the war between the American colonies and the British or would you have mixed feelings as Sarah did?

   • Which group treated Sarah worse—the British or the American patriots?

   • What would have been the most difficult thing to endure about living alone in the wilderness as Sarah did?

   • How would you react if you were charged with witchcraft as Sarah was?

Extension

Read *My Brother Sam Is Dead* by James Lincoln Collier and Christopher Collier. (See TCM 2507 for related activities.) This is a powerful story of the Meeker family, who was caught in the middle of the Revolutionary conflict. The parents opposed the war and supported the British, but the older son Sam ran away to fight in the patriot army. The story is told from the point of view of the younger son Tim, who is uncertain which side is right. This book clearly highlights the heavy cost of war.

Why Don't You Get a Horse, Sam Adams?

This book by Jean Fritz details the life of Sam Adams as a patriot leader, including several of his personality quirks. The reader is introduced to Sam Adams as he walks about town raising the consciousness and anger of his fellow Boston colonists over the behavior and attitudes of their British masters. The book briefly describes the repeated efforts of the British to impose taxes and authority over the rebellious colonists. Sam's involvement in the Boston Tea Party, the Boston Massacre, and Paul Revere's ride are described.

Assignment

Read the book *Why Don't You Get a Horse, Sam Adams?* Then answer the questions below.

1. What did Sam Adams have to do with the Boston Tea Party?

2. How did Sam escape from Lexington when the British were coming to arrest him?

3. Who kept trying to talk Sam into riding a horse?

4. Why did Sam get new clothes?

5. Who taught Sam how to mount a horse?

6. Who was Queue?

7. What happened to Sam's father that made Sam so opposed to British rule?

And Then What Happened, Paul Revere?

Paul Revere was definitely not lazy. This book by Jean Fritz describes the many occupations Paul Revere had in his lifetime and his many contributions to the fight for American independence. The author describes how Revere participated in the Boston Tea Party and his many rides to keep citizens in Massachusetts and other colonies informed of the events in Boston. The reader is even given a glimpse of Revere's forgetfulness and how it almost prevented his most famous ride.

Assignment

Read the book *And Then What Happened, Paul Revere?* Then answer the questions below.

1. What were all the jobs that Revere had?

2. How many days did it take Paul to ride from Boston to Philadelphia and back?

3. How many children did Paul have (including those who died young)?

4. What two things did Paul forget on his famous ride? How did he get them?

5. How long did the British keep Paul in jail?

6. Why did Paul have to walk back to Lexington?

Focus on Author Jean Fritz

Jean Fritz was born to missionary parents in Hankow, China, on November 16, 1915. She was brought up in that city in the midst of massive political upheaval. It was the headquarters of the Communist Party in that part of China and a place filled with danger, intrigue, and many diverse cultural influences. Fritz spoke fluent Chinese, celebrated German Christmas traditions with friends from Germany, played with Italian children, and met people from many nations. She met Chinese warlords, American sailors, Siberian Russians who had escaped the Russian revolution, and many other foreigners who came to visit her parents.

Jean's family was often in danger. Angry peasants once stoned her and her mother as they traveled along a country road. A gang of angry union workers invaded their home and started a riot. She heard battles between police and pirates and often had to be prepared to leave the city in an instant.

Fritz moved to the United States when she was 13 years old. She became deeply appreciative of her nation and the people who created the country. This may account for her lifelong interest in the men and women who shaped the future of the United States. Although she has written historical fiction and autobiographies, she is best known for her children's biographies of important American historical figures, especially those from the Revolutionary War era.

Determined to be a writer, she attended Wheaton College and later worked as a children's librarian. Her first efforts at publishing were unproductive, but she eventually became a successful children's author. She is married with two children and lives in Dobbs Ferry, New York, on the Hudson River.

Fritz is proud of the style, content, and historical accuracy of her books. She looks for amusing details, anecdotes, and human foibles that make that character come alive. For example, she used Sam Adams' inability to ride a horse as a key element in her book *Why Don't You Get a Horse, Sam Adams?* John Hancock's fancy apparel and personal vanity add a human touch to the book *Won't You Sign Here, John Hancock?* Patrick Henry's "sending voice" is a highlight of *Where Was Patrick Henry on the 29th of May?* Paul Revere's many jobs and children provide a human note to *And Then What Happened, Paul Revere?*

Focus on Author Jean Fritz *(cont.)*

Jean Fritz never makes up dialogue. If she uses quotes, those are the exact words actually spoken by the character. She admits that she has an ear for gossip and feels like an eavesdropper listening into the distant past. Fritz often sees herself as a reporter, except that the stories she writes are from long ago. She also sees herself as a historical detective probing for the truth about her subject. She wants her readers to have a sense of the real person, warts and all—not as a hero on a statue. Whether it is Patrick Henry's preference for wearing clean underwear or Benjamin Franklin showing off his wealth, you see real people in Jean Fritz's books.

Assignment

Read one of the books related to colonial life or the American Revolution listed below, and make an oral report to the class about the book. Describe the main character, mention important details about his or her life, and tell any interesting anecdotes or stories you learn.

Biographies by Jean Fritz

And Then What Happened, Paul Revere? Putnam, 1973.

Can't You Make Them Behave, King George? Putnam, 1996.

George Washington's Mother. Putnam, 1992.

The Great Little Madison. Putnam, 1989.

Shh! We're Writing the Constitution. Putnam, 1997.

Traitor: The Case of Benedict Arnold. Puffin, 1989.

What's the Big Idea, Ben Franklin? Putnam, 1976.

Where Do You Think You're Going, Christopher Columbus? Putnam, 1981.

Where Was Patrick Henry on the 29th of May? Putnam, 1975.

Who's That Stepping on Plymouth Rock? Putnam, 1975.

Why Don't You Get a Horse, Sam Adams? Putnam, 1974.

Will You Sign Here, John Hancock? Putnam, 1976.

The Language of the Declaration of Independence

The version of the Declaration of Independence provided on pages 54–56 has been abridged (shortened) with some of the grievances removed (especially those which have been repeated in different ways). Various copies of the Declaration illustrate some differences in punctuation and capitalization because usage had not been standardized in the colonies in the 1700s.

Parts of the Document

The Declaration has three main parts: the preamble, the list of grievances, and the formal announcement of independence by the colonies. The preamble is an introduction, which expresses the universal ideas about mankind and government upon which the declaration is based. The list of grievances details all of the offenses of the British government as they are perceived by the American colonists. The concluding announcement of independence is the formal statement that the colonists are no longer under British rule.

Words, Terms, and Expressions

a right inestimable to them—a right beyond any price

absolute Despotism—absolute rule by a tyrant

absolved from all allegiance—no longer connected by citizenship

assent—approval

British brethren—British citizens

candid world—honest observers

consanguinity—having the same ancestry and heritage

consent of the governed—the people accept the rule of law

contract alliances—make treaties with other nations

dissolved Representative Houses—ordered legislatures closed

Divine Providence—God

domestic insurrections—riots

eat out their substance—money (taxes) needed by the people

endowed—given by birth

establish commerce—start businesses

formidable—needed or used (in this usage)

hath shewn—has shown

legislatures—places where free men make laws

levy war—declare war

light and transient causes—frivolous reasons

manly firmness—courage

plundered—destroyed and looted

quartering troops—stationing troops in homes and villages

ravaged—destroyed and ruined

rectitude—strict honesty and moral character

standing armies—soldiers stationed near or in a town

Supreme Judge of the World—God

tenure—length of time

trial by jury—the right to a fair trial

unalienable—cannot be taken away (today *inalienable*)

usurpations—taking power by force

Readers' Theater Notes

Readers' Theater is drama without costumes, props, stage, or memorization. It can be done in the classroom by groups of students who become the cast of the dramatic reading.

Staging

Place four stools, chairs, or desks in a semicircle at the front of the classroom or in a separate stage area. Generally no costumes are used in this type of dramatization, but students dressed in similar clothing or colors can add a nice effect. Props are unnecessary.

Script

Each member of the group should have a clearly marked, useable script of the Declaration of Independence. Practice several times before presenting this to the class.

Performing

Performers should enter the classroom quietly and seriously. They should sit silently without moving and wait with heads lowered. The first reader should begin, and the other readers should focus on whoever is reading, except when they are performing.

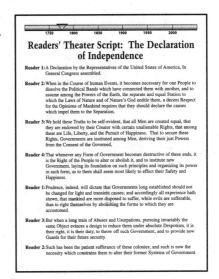

Assignment

1. Practice the Readers' Theater Script for the Declaration of Independence (pages 54–56), which is an abridged version of the text. Work as a group to prepare for the performance.

2. Carefully study the Language of the Declaration activity on page 52. Note the meanings of unfamiliar words and phrases.

Extension

- Practice reading the Declaration of Independence with some background music playing, such as an instrumental version of a patriotic song.

- Present your dramatic reading to another class or at Open House, Loved Ones' Day, or some other special school event.

- Find a copy of the *Declaration of Sentiments* written by Elizabeth Cady Stanton and modeled on the Declaration of Independence. This document became an important milestone in the history of women's efforts to secure equal rights. Use the Internet or books devoted to women's rights to find a copy. Prepare a dramatic reading of this document. Girls could dress in the long dresses of the 1840s.

Readers' Theater Script: The Declaration of Independence

Reader 1: A Declaration by the Representatives of the United States of America, In General Congress assembled.

Reader 2: When in the Course of human Events, it becomes necessary for one People to dissolve the Political Bands which have connected them with another, and to assume among the Powers of the Earth, the separate and equal Station to which the Laws of Nature and of Nature's God entitle them, a decent Respect for the Opinions of Mankind requires that they should declare the causes which impel them to the Separation.

Reader 3: We hold these Truths to be self-evident, that all Men are created equal, that they are endowed by their Creator with certain unalienable Rights, that among these are Life, Liberty, and the Pursuit of Happiness. That to secure these Rights, Governments are instituted among Men, deriving their just Powers from the Consent of the Governed.

Reader 4: That whenever any Form of Government becomes destructive of these ends, it is the Right of the People to alter or abolish it, and to institute new Government, laying its foundation on such principles and organizing its power in such form, as to them shall seem most likely to effect their Safety and Happiness.

Reader 1: Prudence, indeed, will dictate that Governments long established should not be changed for light and transient causes; and accordingly all experience hath shewn, that mankind are more disposed to suffer, while evils are sufferable, than to right themselves by abolishing the forms to which they are accustomed.

Reader 3: But when a long train of Abuses and Usurpations, pursuing invariably the same Object evinces a design to reduce them under absolute Despotism, it is their right, it is their duty, to throw off such Government, and to provide new Guards for their future security.

Reader 2: Such has been the patient sufferance of these colonies; and such is now the necessity which constrains them to alter their former Systems of Government.

Readers' Theater Script: The Declaration of Independence *(cont.)*

Reader 4: The History of the present King of Great Britain is a history of repeated Injuries and Usurpations, all having in direct object the establishment of an absolute Tyranny over these States.

Reader 1: To prove this, let Facts be submitted to a candid World.

Reader 2: He has refused his Assent to Laws, the most wholesome and necessary for the public Good.

Reader 3: He has forbidden his Governors to pass Laws of immediate and pressing importance, unless suspended in their operation till his Assent should be obtained; and when so suspended, he has utterly neglected to attend to them.

Reader 4: He has refused to pass other Laws for the accommodation of large districts of people, unless those people would relinquish the right of Representation in the Legislature, a right inestimable to them and formidable to tyrants only . . .

Reader 3: He has dissolved Representative Houses repeatedly, for opposing with manly firmness his invasions on the rights of the people . . .

Reader 1: He has made Judges dependent on his Will alone, for the tenure of their offices, and the amount and payment of their salaries.

Reader 2: He has erected a multitude of New Offices, and sent hither swarms of Officers to harass our people, and eat out their substance.

Reader 3: He has kept among us, in times of peace, Standing Armies without the Consent of our legislatures . . .

Reader 4: For quartering large bodies of armed troops among us . . .

Reader 1: For cutting off our Trade with all parts of the world:

Reader 3: For imposing Taxes on us without our Consent:

Readers' Theater Script: The Declaration of Independence *(cont.)*

Reader 2: For depriving us, in many cases, of the benefits of Trial by Jury . . .

Reader 3: For suspending our own Legislatures, and declaring themselves invested with power to legislate for us in all cases whatsoever . . .

Reader 1: He has plundered our Seas, ravaged our Coasts, burnt our towns, and destroyed the Lives of our People . . .

Reader 4: He has excited domestic insurrections amongst us, and had endeavoured to bring on the inhabitants of our frontiers, the merciless Indian Savages, whose known Rule of Warfare is an undistinguished Destruction of all Ages, Sexes and Conditions . . .

Reader 2: Nor have we been wanting in attentions to our British brethren . . .They too have been deaf to the Voice of Justice and Consanguinity. We must, therefore . . . hold them as we hold the rest of mankind, Enemies in War, in Peace Friends.

Reader 4: We, therefore, the Representatives of the United States of America, in General Congress, Assembled, appealing to the Supreme Judge of the world for the Rectitude of our Intentions, do, in the Name, and by the Authority of the good People of these Colonies, solemnly Publish and Declare,

Reader 3: That these United Colonies are, and of Right ought to be, Free and Independent States; that they are Absolved from all Allegiance to the British Crown, and that all political connection between them and the State of Great Britain, is and ought to be totally dissolved;

Reader 2: And that as Free and Independent States, they have full Power to levy War, conclude Peace, contract Alliances, establish Commerce, and do all other Acts and Things which Independent States may of right do.

Reader 1: And for the support of this Declaration, with a firm Reliance on the Protection of Divine Providence, we mutually pledge to each other our Lives, our Fortunes, and our sacred Honor.

Teacher Lesson Plans for Social Studies

Using Time Lines

Objectives: Students will learn to derive information from a time line and make time lines relevant to them.

Materials: copies of Time Line of the Revolution (pages 59 and 60); research resources including books, encyclopedias, atlases, almanacs, and Internet sites

Procedure

1. Collect resources for your students so that they have plenty of places to find information.

2. Review the concept of a time line, using the school year as an example.

3. Reproduce and distribute the Time Line of the Revolution (pages 59 and 60) activity sheets. Review the various events listed on the time line.

4. If desired, have students place 10 additional dates on the time line as described in the first Extension activity on page 60. Students can use the articles from the beginning of this book to locate these. As an alternate or additional assignment, have students create their own visual time lines as described in the second Extension activity on page 60.

Assessment: Have students share their additional dates and visual time lines with the class.

Using Maps

Objective: Students will learn to use and derive information from a variety of maps.

Materials: copies of Map of the Colonies in 1775 (page 61); copies of Fighting the Revolutionary War (page 62); copies of The United States in 1783 (page 63); atlases, almanacs, and other maps for reference and comparison

Procedure

1. Review Map of the Colonies in 1775 (page 61). Point out important features of the map to students. Have students use the map to complete the assignment.

2. Review Fighting the Revolutionary War (page 62). Have students complete the assignment on the page.

3. Review the Map of the United States in 1783 (page 63). Have students complete the assignment on the page.

Assessment: Correct the map activity pages together. Check students' understanding, and review the basic concepts.

Teacher Lesson Plans for Social Studies *(cont.)*

Researching the Revolution

Objectives: Students will develop skills in finding, organizing, and presenting research information.

Materials: copies of Researching the Causes of the Revolutionary War (page 64); copies of Researching Revolutionary War Battles (page 65); copies of Researching Heroes and Heroines of the Revolution (pages 66 and 67); books, encyclopedias, and Internet sources

Procedure

1. Review the information on Researching the Causes of the Revolutionary War (page 64). Emphasize the need to organize material and the type of information required. Assign each student a cause to research. Review the research reminders.

2. Review the information on Researching Revolutionary War Battles (page 65). Stress the need to take notes in an organized manner, the kinds of information required for each battle, potential sources to use, and review the research reminders on page 64. Assign a battle to each student or pair of students.

3. Review the information on Researching Heroes and Heroines of the Revolution (pages 66 and 67). Review the guidelines with your class. Point out the different sources of information you have collected. Review the research reminders on page 64. Let students select the person they want to write about from the list on page 67.

4. Allow time for students to prepare their reports. Schedule time for presentations so students can share the information with the class.

Assessment: Assess students on the basis of their written reports and oral classroom presentations.

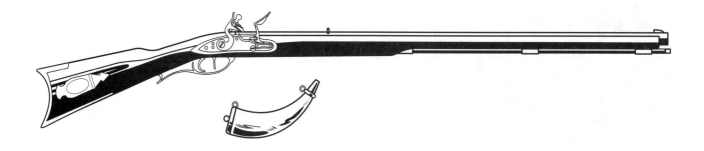

Time Line of the Revolution

1763—Great Britain wins the French and Indian War.
The Proclamation of 1763 closes the lands west of the Appalachian Mountains to settlers.

1764—The Sugar Act is passed to raise taxes from the colonies.

1765—The Stamp Act is passed to collect taxes on paper goods.

1766—Organized resistance forces repeal of the Stamp Act.

1767—The Townshend Acts are passed to tax glass, tea, paper, and other products.

1770—American boycotts and resistance to Townshend Acts forces repeal of all but the tea tax.
The Boston Massacre inflames tensions in the colonies.

1772—Sam Adams organizes the Committees of Correspondence to coordinate anti-British actions in the colonies.

1773—The Tea Act is passed giving British merchants a monopoly on the sale of tea to the colonies.
The Sons of Liberty dump tea off a British ship at the Boston Tea Party.

1774—The Intolerable Acts are passed to punish Boston for the Boston Tea Party.
The First Continental Congress meets to discuss the growing crisis.

1775—The Battles of Lexington and Concord signal the beginning of the war.
The Battle of Bunker Hill is fought.
The Second Continental Congress meets and Washington is named commander in chief of the Continental Army.

1776—The Declaration of Independence is declared on July 4.
The British win the Battle of Long Island and occupy New York City.
Washington crosses the Delaware and defeats the British at Trenton.

1777—The Americans win a major battle at Saratoga.
Washington's forces spend the winter at Valley Forge.

1778—The French become allies, sending men and munitions.

1779—John Paul Jones defeats the British ship *Serapis*.

1780—American traitor Benedict Arnold escapes before he can hand over West Point to the British.

1781—British General Cornwallis is surrounded by American and French troops and bottled up at Yorktown by French ships. His surrender effectively ends the war.

1783—The final peace treaty grants American colonies their independence from Great Britain.

Time Line of the Revolution *(cont.)*

Assignment

Study the time line on page 59. Use the Internet, textbooks, encyclopedias, almanacs, and other sources to look up the dates for each of the following events that occurred in the Revolutionary era. Then insert these dates and facts on the time line.

- The Currency Act forbids the American colonies from creating their own money.
- The Quartering Act requires the colonies to provide food and shelter for British troops.
- Thomas Paine publishes *Common Sense*, rallying Americans to the cause of revolution.
- Washington wins the battle of Princeton.
- The Articles of Confederation are adopted by the Continental Congress.
- George Rogers Clark captures Vincennes and controls much of the west.
- "Mad" Anthony Wayne captures Stony Point for the Americans.
- Americans win a major battle at King's Mountain, South Carolina.

Extension

1. Find at least 10 events in American history to add to the time line on page 59. They can include wars, inventions, presidential elections, disasters, or sporting events and may be before, during, or after the dates currently listed on the time line. List these dates in chronological order to share with the class. Be sure you know a little background information about each additional event.

2. Create a visual time line by adding photos, clip art, or drawings to go along with the facts you found. Use poster board or tape sheets of paper together, and draw the time line. Then write the dates and events on the line, and add the illustrations. Use colored pencils or markers to make it more colorful.

1750   1800   1850   1900   1950   2000

Map of the Colonies in 1775

The 13 American colonies that declared independence from Great Britain were located along the edge of the Atlantic Ocean with the Appalachian Mountains at their western edge. Most of the rest of the continent was controlled either by the British, French, or Spanish and occupied by unfriendly Native Americans.

Assignment

List the 13 American colonies from north to south.

1. _____

2. _____

3. _____

4. _____

5. _____

6. _____

7. _____

8. _____

9. _____

10. _____

11. _____

12. _____

13. _____

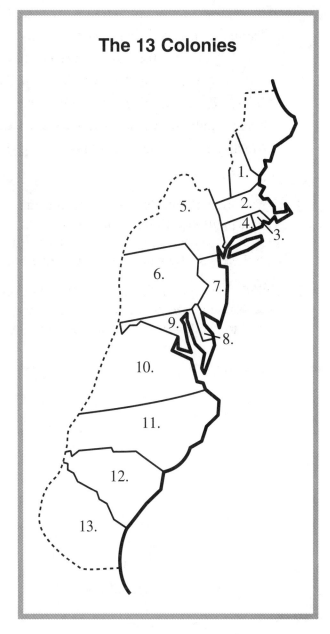

The 13 Colonies

Fighting the Revolutionary War

Many momentous battles were fought in the American Revolutionary War between 1775 and 1781. Although the American forces lost far more battles than they won, the cost of the war finally forced Great Britain to agree to independence and peace.

Assignment

Read pages 17–26 to find out where each of the following battles was fought and the year in which it took place.

Battle	**Colony**	**Year**
1. Brandywine Creek	_____	_____
2. Bunker Hill (Breed's Hill)	_____	_____
3. Camden	_____	_____
4. Charleston	_____	_____
5. Concord	_____	_____
6. Cowpens	_____	_____
7. Guilford Courthouse	_____	_____
8. King's Mountain	_____	_____
9. Lexington	_____	_____
10. Long Island	_____	_____
11. Monmouth	_____	_____
12. Princeton	_____	_____
13. Saratoga	_____	_____
14. Savannah	_____	_____
15. Ticonderoga	_____	_____
16. Trenton	_____	_____
17. Vincennes	_____	_____
18. Yorktown	_____	_____

Answer the following questions.

19. Which was the first battle of the war?_____

20. Which was the last major battle of the war? _____

21. Which battle was important because it convinced the French government to send aid to the

     Americans? _____

The United States in 1783

The Treaty of Paris in 1783 provided a very generous land settlement for the new United States. In addition to the original 13 colonies, the new nation received all of the land between the Great Lakes and Spanish Florida and between the original colonies and the Mississippi River.

Assignment

On the map below, label the following:

1. 13 original states
2. Atlantic Ocean
3. Gulf of Mexico

4. Mississippi River
5. Ohio River
6. five Great Lakes

Researching the Causes of the Revolutionary War

There were several British actions that led to the American Revolution. Choose one of the following causes and write a research paper about it. Refer to the notes at the bottom to help you.

- Proclamation of 1763
- Sugar Act
- Stamp Act
- Quartering Act

- Declaratory Act
- Townshend Acts
- Tea Act
- Intolerable Acts

Use the questions listed below as guidelines to help you write an effective report.

1. What law or command did the British make?
2. What were the stipulations (requirements) of the law?
3. Why did the British do what they did?
4. What year did the action occur?
5. Which British leader or leaders was responsible for the action?
6. Why were people in the colonies upset?
7. Which colony or colonies was most affected by the British action?
8. Which colonial leaders and groups were involved in resisting the British action?
9. What actions did the colonial leaders take in response to the British law?
10. How did the behavior of the colonies influence the British? (For example: Did laws get changed? Did the British respond with force?)
11. How did this British action lead to the American Revolution?

Writing a Report

When writing a report, it is important to do the following:

- Use as many sources as possible, including textbooks, encyclopedias, Internet Web sites, and books about the American Revolution.
- Take notes carefully.
- Don't use complete sentences in notes.
- Get all of the facts.
- Use your own words. Don't copy sentences word for word.
- Arrange the notes in order by time and place.
- Check spelling, especially of unfamiliar names and places.
- Make a final copy in paragraph format.
- Carefully check punctuation, margins, neatness, and other writing conventions.

1750 1800 1850 1900 1950 2000

Researching Revolutionary War Battles

Choose one of the following battles, and write a research paper about it. Take notes before you begin writing the report. See Writing a Report (page 64) for research reminders.

Revolutionary War Battles

- Bennington
- *Bonhomme Richard* vs. *Serapis* (sea battle)
- Brandywine
- Bunker Hill
- Camden
- Concord
- Charleston
- Cowpens

- Fort Ticonderoga
- Germantown
- Guilford Courthouse
- Kaskaskia
- King's Mountain
- Lexington
- Long Island
- Monmouth
- Montreal

- Princeton
- Quebec
- Saratoga
- Savannah
- Trenton
- Vincennes
- White Plains
- Yorktown

Use the information listed below as a guideline to help you write an effective report.

1. Date of the battle
2. Place of the battle (colony, city, town, river, etc.)
3. Length of the battle in days
4. Generals in charge of each army
5. Important leaders involved in the actual battle
6. Numbers of fighting men on each side
7. Problems faced by the British
8. Problems faced by the Americans
9. Weapons used by each side

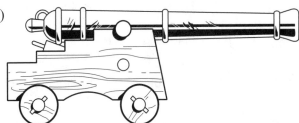

10. Special acts of bravery during the battle (leading a charge, fighting against a vastly superior number, etc.)
11. How the battle came about (What was each army trying to do?)
12. The influence of weather and terrain (the shape of the land)
13. Results of the battle (who won, effect on public morale)

Extension

Draw a map illustrating the battle that you researched. Show where each army began the battle. Use arrows to show the direction of the fight. Include all the information you can about the battle on the map.

Researching Heroes and Heroines of the American Revolution

Choose a Revolutionary War hero or heroine from the list on the next page. Use the research outline below to learn everything you can about this person. Use encyclopedias, almanacs, biographies, the Internet, and other sources of information to find out important dates and information about his or her personal life. Become familiar with your hero's or heroine's accomplishments.

Take notes, and write down the basic facts in an organized way, such as noted in the outline below. See Writing a Report (page 64) for research reminders.

I. Youth
   A. Birth place and date
   B. Home life and experiences
   C. Schooling (if any)
   D. Childhood heroes
   E. Interesting facts or stories about the person's youth

II. Revolutionary War Experiences
   A. Reasons for independence
      1. Why your person disliked Great Britain
      2. Influential people in his or her life
      3. Your hero's personal arguments for freedom

   B. Participation in the rebellion
      1. Battles fought or positions held
      2. Important things done before the war
      3. Important things done during the war
      4. Adventures and experiences before and during the war
      5. Friends and companions

   C. Lifestyle and personal habits
      1. Values he or she believed in
      2. Was your hero a risk-taker or cautious? (give examples)
      3. Personal behavior (cruel, kind, honest, etc.)
      4. Leadership experiences
      5. Physical abilities and disabilities (illnesses, physical problems)

III. Death
   A. Date of death
   B. Age at death
   C. Cause of death (facts about the death)

Researching Heroes and Heroines of the American Revolution (cont.)

Below is a partial list of American Revolutionary War heroes and heroines.

Advocates of Rebellion

Abigail Adams—told husband to "remember the ladies"

Benjamin Franklin—inventor; diplomat; patriotic leader

Crispus Attucks—African-American victim of Boston Massacre

Esther Reed—fundraiser and proponent of freedom

James Otis—radical proponent of rebellion

John Adams—lawyer; avid supporter of independence

John Hancock—wealthy merchant and public leader

Lydia Darragh—Quaker girl who spied for Washington's army

Mary Katherine Goddard—successful publisher and patriot

Mercy Otis Warren—historian, advocate of independence

Patience Wright—wax figure artist; American spy in London

Patrick Henry—said "Give me liberty or give me death"

Paul Revere—silversmith; Son of Liberty; messenger

Phillis Wheatley—slave poet; voice for liberty

Sam Adams—"Father of the American Revolution"

Sybil Ludington—16-year-old spy and courier

Thomas Jefferson—primary author of the Declaration of Independence

Thomas Paine—*Common Sense* writer who promoted revolution

Soldiers

Alexander Hamilton—aide to General Washington

Benedict Arnold—American hero turned traitor

Charles Lee—disobedient general who became a traitor

Jean Baptiste Rochambeau—French commander who helped win at Yorktown

Daniel Morgan—superb leader of a company of riflemen

Deborah Sampson—secret soldier

Francis Marion—nicknamed the "Swamp Fox"

General Horatio Gates—a hero at Saratoga

George Rogers Clark—western warrior

George Washington—commander in chief of the American forces

Henry Lee—"Light-Horse Harry" was a great soldier and writer

John Paul Jones—American naval commander

Margaret Corbin—fired her husband's cannon after he was killed

Marquis de Lafayette—French war hero; Washington's friend

Mary "Molly" Hays—took her husband's place at the cannon

Nathan Hale—U.S. spy who gave his life for his country

Nathanael Greene—wealthy war hero who gave all for freedom

British Leaders

Ann Lee—religious leader; British supporter

Banastre Tarleton—brutal, driven, brilliant officer

General Charles Cornwallis—defeated at Yorktown

General John Burgoyne—"Gentleman Johnny"; lost at Saratoga

General Thomas Gage—commander of British forces in Boston

George III—unyielding King of England

Joseph Brant—Iroquois ally of the British

Mary Jemison—caught between three cultures

Peggy Arnold—Benedict Arnold's American wife and British spy

Sir Henry Clinton—British commander in America

William Franklin—Benjamin Franklin's son and a British loyalist

Teacher Lesson Plans for Science

Franklin and Jefferson: Scientists

Objectives: Students will replicate simple science projects related to the studies of Benjamin Franklin and Thomas Jefferson.

Materials: copies of Ben Franklin: Scientist (page 69); copies of Working with Static Electricity (page 70); copies of The Inventors: Franklin and Jefferson (page 71); copies of Creating an Invention (page 72); copies of Thomas Jefferson: Botanist (page 73); science materials listed on each page (including clear plastic cups, masking tape, bare copper wire, aluminum foil, manila folders, scissors, pushpins, sandpaper, paper plates, salt, pepper, balloons, paper towels, birdseed, Styrofoam trays or plates, tissue, glitter, or dried parsley flakes)

Procedure

1. Collect the materials listed on each page before assigning each project.

2. Reproduce and distribute the Ben Franklin: Scientist (page 69) and Working with Static Electricity (page 70) activity sheets. Review the information on Franklin, distribute the necessary materials, and read the directions for making and using the electroscope with the class. Also distribute the materials and demonstrate the procedures for "unpeppering" the salt on page 70.

3. Reproduce and distribute The Inventors: Franklin and Jefferson (page 71) and Creating an Invention (page 72) activity sheets. Review the information on Franklin and Jefferson. Brainstorm possible inventions that are needed, and review the directions for completing the list of complicated and simple inventions on page 71. Brainstorm the invention ideas on page 72. Encourage students to create an invention idea, design it, and make a model from everyday materials. Help students assess the success of their inventions.

4. Reproduce and distribute Thomas Jefferson: Botanist (page 73). Review the information on Jefferson. Distribute the wild birdseed and other materials needed. Have students examine the birdseed and then plant it hydroponically as described on the work sheet. Allow students to examine and sketch the seeds daily for about 10 days.

Assessment: Have students share their inventions and science experiences with the class in a scientific colloquium during which students also ask questions and relate their experiences to those of other classmates.

Ben Franklin: Scientist

Ben Franklin was the most famous American in the world during the late 1700s. He was as well known and admired for his scientific interests as for his efforts in creating a new nation. Franklin's famous kite experiment proved that lightning is a form of static electricity. He once used a Leyden jar that could store static electricity to electrocute a turkey and to give an electrical shock to his friends.

Making an Electroscope

Below are directions for making an electroscope, which can be used to detect the presence of a static charge.

Materials: clear plastic cup, masking tape, 3-inch piece of bare copper wire, aluminum foil, manila folder, scissors, pushpin, sandpaper, balloon

Procedure

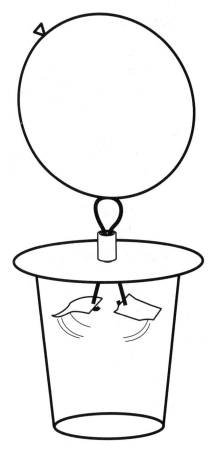

1. Cut a piece of manila folder to make a round cover for the clear plastic cup.

2. Use the sandpaper or scissors to scrape the plastic coating from a 3-inch piece of copper wire if it is not already bare.

3. Use the pushpin to make a small hole in the center of the lid that you cut out.

4. Make a loop with the wire, and push the pointed end of the wire through the hole so that it extends down about one inch. Put a piece of masking tape around the wire near the hole so that it does not slip.

5. Fold the two prongs of wire up in opposite directions.

6. Cut out two small, square centimeter pieces of aluminum foil.

7. Use the pushpin to make a hole at the top of each piece of foil. Hook one piece of foil on each wire hook.

8. Tape the lid tightly onto the plastic cup.

Using the Electroscope

1. Inflate the balloon, and tie it closed. Rub the balloon about 30 times in one direction only along your hair, sweater, or clothing. This should create a static charge.

2. With the balloon, touch the loop of wire above the cup.

3. Observe the pieces of foil. They should push apart because they are both receiving the same charge. Like charges repel each other just as the same poles of a magnet repel each other.

4. Hold the balloon next to the plastic cup, and notice how the foil pieces are attracted toward the balloon.

Working With Static Electricity

Unpeppering the Salt

Materials: paper plate, salt, pepper, balloon, glitter or dried parsley flakes, tissue

Procedure

1. Pour a teaspoon of salt onto a paper plate.

2. Next pour some pepper onto the plate, and mix the salt and pepper together.

3. Inflate the balloon, and tie it closed. Rub the balloon about 30 times in one direction only along your hair, sweater, or clothing. (Do not go back and forth.) This should create a static charge.

4. Hold the balloon above the plate with the salt and pepper. Observe what happens to the pepper.

5. Did some of the salt also get attracted to the balloon?

6. Watch the bits of pepper on the balloon. Do any of them appear to leap off?

7. What happens when a friend holds a balloon next to yours? Do any of the flakes move? Do the balloons move?

8. Add some glitter, dried parsley flakes, or other types of flakes to the plate. Does the balloon pick them up?

9. Tear up pieces of tissue, and put them on the plate. Can the balloon pick these up? Will the balloon pick up larger pieces of tissue?

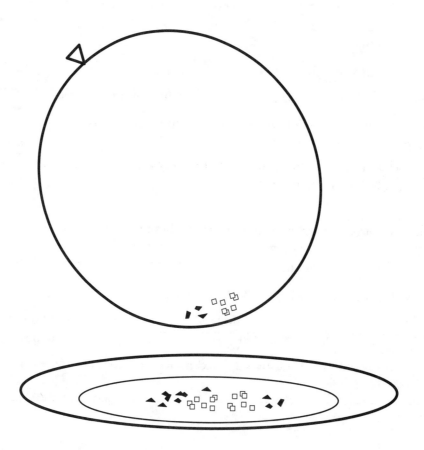

The Inventors: Franklin and Jefferson

Ben Franklin was renowned for practical and useful inventions. He invented bifocal glasses so that he could see better. The Franklin stove was a vast improvement over the fireplace and earlier stoves because it kept the heat centralized. The lightning rod saved countless homes from being burned down by lightning strikes.

Thomas Jefferson wrote the Declaration of Independence on a portable desk he designed and built himself. He invented a gadget to copy letters as he wrote them. He invented a dumbwaiter, which is a kind of elevator for bringing food and drinks up from the basement. His invention of a better plow greatly improved farmers' lives.

People often wish that some tool or gadget existed to make work easier or life more interesting. Many inventions, like Jefferson's plow or Franklin's glasses, are improvements on previous inventions or designs. Some inventions, like the computer or the television, combine many ideas and inventions from many people. Others are quite simple.

Assignment

List six inventions that are very complicated and combine the ideas and inventions of many people.

1. _____

2. _____

3. _____

4. _____

5. _____

6. _____

List six inventions that are very simple and combine only a few ideas. Think of toys, gadgets, and basic, uncomplicated tools and equipment.

1. _____

2. _____

3. _____

4. _____

5. _____

6. _____

Creating an Invention

Think of all the ideas you have ever thought of for an invention. These may include toys, computer games, vehicles, sporting equipment, clothing, animal care products, spy apparatus, and other ideas. List some of your ideas below and how each would be used. Then choose one of the inventions, and draw a small sketch of it on a separate sheet of paper.

Invention Ideas   **Use for the Invention**

1. _____   _____

2. _____   _____

3. _____   _____

4. _____   _____

5. _____   _____

6. _____   _____

7. _____   _____

8. _____   _____

9. _____   _____

10. _____   _____

Extension

Nearly all inventors make a small model of their design before they build a full-size version. Select one of your simple inventions to work on. List the materials you will need, collect the components, and build a prototype. Then write a brief summary of the experience, using the following guidelines.

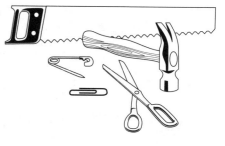

1. Describe your final product.

2. What materials did you need to build the prototype?

3. Does the model work?

4. Did you have any problems building the model? If so, how did you solve them?

5. What could you do to improve the model?

Thomas Jefferson: Botanist

Thomas Jefferson was extremely interested in the science of growing plants. He was one of the first Americans to grow tomatoes for food as well as for decoration. He often filled his pockets with the seeds of different kinds of wheat, rice, and other grains when he traveled abroad. He planted these seeds when he returned home and raised crops that were more productive.

Growing Plants from Seeds

1. Study the wild birdseed or other seeds provided by your teacher. Separate seeds of different shapes and sizes into different piles.

2. Place a double thickness of paper towel in a Styrofoam tray or on a plastic-coated paper plate.

3. Use a spray bottle or slowly pour water to make the paper towel damp, but not soaked. Pour off any excess water.

4. Arrange your seeds on the paper towel in small patches according to the different piles you made. Make sure the seeds are separated from each other.

5. Cover the seeds with one layer of damp paper towel.

6. Carefully lift the paper towel off the seeds after one day. Examine the seeds, using a magnifying glass if you have one. Have the seeds started to swell? Have any of them started to sprout?

7. Examine the seeds every day. Observe the stages of growth.

8. Keep track of the following information:

   a. How many seeds of each type sprouted?

   b. How many seeds of each type failed to sprout or just got moldy?

9. What percentage of seeds sprouted? (Divide the number of seeds that sprouted by the total number of seeds you started with.)

10. Describe the results of this experiment. Draw sketches to illustrate your observations.

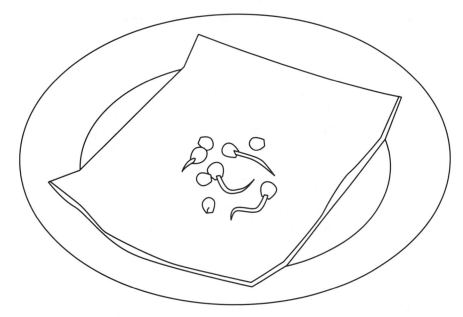

Culminating Activities for History Day

Set aside one day to be devoted to activities related to your study of the American Revolution. If possible, do the activity with two or three classes at the same grade level. This allows you to share some of the burdens and provides a special experience for the entire grade level.

Costumes

Encourage your students to come in costumes that look like the colonial or early national period. Encourage students to wear leather shoes, boots, or moccasins instead of tennis shoes. The Jean Fritz books offer many illustrations that are especially useful for boys. Long socks pulled up over pants will work well as will a white, dress shirt and a man's long dark suit coat. A handkerchief or piece of lace fabric can be used for the ruffles at the neck. Long dresses from female relatives will often work for the girls.

Parent Help

Encourage parents or adult family members to come for all or part of the day to enjoy the proceedings and also help set up and monitor the activities. Check with parents to discover any special talents, interests, or hobbies that would be a match for specific centers.

Eat Hearty

If you have parent volunteers, plan a luncheon with a Revolutionary theme. Parents and students could do the decorations (red/white/blue) together at one of the centers. Most students today are far pickier than their Revolutionary counterparts, but you might choose two or three dishes with a colonial flavor.

Setting Up Centers

The centers you set up should relate in some way to the American Revolution, daily life during that time, or activities you did using this book. Centers should allow small groups of six or seven students to participate. Each center should take about 20 minutes. Students should then rotate to the next activity.

The following suggestions will get you started. You can add any others for which you have special expertise.

❑ **A Discussion Center**

At this center students could argue the pros and cons of separating from Britain. Students should be divided into two sides—one to recommend independence and the other to continue under British rule. For ideas and information, they could use the reading selection and research activity on the causes of the war found in this book.

❑ **Poetry in Two Voices and Readers' Theater**

In a poetry center, students could team with a partner and prepare one of the narrative poems in this book for presentation to an audience. The readers' theater center would involve practicing a script with a small group for a presentation.

Culminating Activities for History Day *(cont.)*

Setting Up Centers *(cont.)*

❑ **Constructing Colonial Homes and Villages**

Students at this center could construct colonial homes, farms, and buildings using modeling clay, craft sticks, sand, small pieces of fabric, construction paper, and other art supplies. For reference, students would need books or pictures of colonial structures in various colonies. The buildings could even be arranged into villages.

❑ **Frontier Games**

Frontier games included foot races, variations of hide and seek, rolling hoops, flying kites, and snap the whip. A soccer-type of kicking game was played in some localities. Toys included tops and marbles. A sports center could feature relay races and one-on-one contests between students in the group. You could use hula-hoops instead of barrel hoops and have students race while rolling the hoops. A separate center could feature some of the smaller games or toys mentioned above.

❑ **Map Making**

A variety of maps could be made at this center. Maps of battles or colonies would be appropriate. Use the map section of this book for examples, and find others in atlases, encyclopedias, and on the Internet. Small groups of two or three students could create these maps on tagboard, large construction paper, or in three-dimensional form using clay or salt and flour.

❑ **Clay Figures or Busts**

In this center, students could use modeling or sculpting clay to make figures or busts of some of the Revolutionary heroes and heroines they have studied. A 25-pound bag of sculpting clay can be divided into 18 or more rectangular blocks of clay with a piece of fishing line. Use toothpicks, craft sticks, or plastic knives to carve the features. Have paper towels available for cleanup.

❑ **Other Centers**

Other centers could include learning a square dance, weaving a simple pattern with yarn, knot tying, or a simple woodworking project.

Annotated Bibliography

Fiction

Collier, James Lincoln, and Christopher Collier. *My Brother Sam Is Dead.* Scholastic, 1974. (Classic story of the personal conflict in choosing sides during the war.)

Duey, Kathleen. *Mary Alice Peale: Philadelphia, 1777.* Aladdin, 1996. (Well-written account in diary form of a family torn apart by the war.)

Gregory, Kristiana. *The Winter of Red Snow: The Revolutionary War Diary of Abigail Jane Stewart.* Scholastic, 1996. (Child's-eye view of the winter at Valley Forge.)

Nonfiction

Adams, Russell B., ed. *The Revolutionaries.* Time-Life, Inc., 1996. (Superior, detailed account of the war for excellent readers.)

Dolan, Edward F. *The American Revolution: How We Fought the War of Independence.* Millbrook Press, 1995. (Clear, concise account of the actual fighting during the Revolution.)

Egger-Bovet, Howard, and Marlene Smith-Baranzini. *U.S. Kids History: Book of the American Revolution.* Little, Brown, 1994. (Collection of sidelights, games, and stories about the war.)

Fink, Sam. *The Declaration of Independence: The Words That Made America.* Scholastic, 2002. (The text of the Declaration is delightfully illustrated.)

Fradin, Dennis Brindell. *The Signers: The Fifty-six Stories Behind the Declaration of Independence.* Walker, 2002. (An excellent account of the lives and intentions of the 56 men who signed the Declaration.)

Furstinger, Nancy. *The Boston Tea Party.* Bridgestone Books, 2002. (A brief, accurate account of the event in easy-to-read prose.)

Gourley, Catherine. *Welcome to Felicity's World 1774.* Pleasant Company, 1999. (An account of the life and times in the colonies just before hostilities from a child's level of interest.)

Masoff, Joy. *American Revolution.* Scholastic, 2000. (Vignettes about the people and times from the Chronicles of America series.)

Meltzer, Milton, ed. *The American Revolutionaries: A History in Their Own Words.* Crowell, 1987. (Personal reflections and accounts from average citizens affected by the war.)

Murphy, Jim. *A Young Patriot: The American Revolution as Experienced by One Boy.* Clarion, 1996. (The Revolution told from the point of view of a soldier in Washington's army.)

Oberle, Lora Polack. *The Declaration of Independence.* Bridgestone Books, 2002. (A brief, accurate, easy-to-understand account of the events surrounding the Declaration.)

Annotated Bibliography *(cont.)*

Nonfiction *(cont.)*

O'Neill, Laurie A. *The Boston Tea Party.* Millbrook, 1996. (A solid, detailed account of the events leading up to the Revolution.)

Stefoff, Rebecca. *Revolutionary War.* Marshall Cavendish, 2001. (Brief account of the battles with exceptional maps.)

Zeinert, Karen. *Those Remarkable Women of the American Revolution.* Millbrook, 1996. (Fascinating vignettes from the feminine side of the Revolution.)

Zell, Fran. *A Multicultural Portrait of the American Revolution.* Marshall Cavendish, 1996. (Stories of women, Native Americans, and African-Americans during the Revolution.)

Picture Book

Penner, Lucille Recht. *The Liberty Tree: The Beginning of the American Revolution.* Random House, 1998. (Colorfully illustrated, brief account of the events leading up to the Declaration.)

Poetry

Burns, Marjorie, ed. *Casey at the Bat and Other Poems to Perform.* Scholastic, 1990. (Poems that students can recite and act out.)

Burns, Marjorie, ed. *The Charge of the Light Brigade and Other Story Poems.* Scholastic, 1990. (Ballads and story poems to use for two persons.)

Glossary

agriculture—farming and raising crops

allies—people or nations on the same side of a war

boycott—refusing to buy goods in order to force acceptance of demands

casualties—persons killed or wounded in a war

cavalry—soldiers fighting on horseback

colony—a group of settlers in a distant land under the control of another nation

correspondence—writing letters

debtors—people who can be imprisoned for owing money

emigration—leaving one country to settle in another

haven—a place of safety for religious or political dissidents

Hessians—German soldiers hired by the British

indentured servant—person owing several years of service to another person

insurrection—act of rebellion against the government

intolerable—unbearable

legislature—a place where representatives make laws

Loyalist—person loyal to Britain and King George III

massacre—the murder of many people

militia—a group of local citizen soldiers

Minutemen—American citizens ready to fight at a moment's notice

monopoly—complete control of the sale of a product

morale—sense of courage and hope

Parliament—Britain's law-making assembly

patriot—an American colonist who favored independence

proclamation—an official declaration

quartering—forcing families to feed and house soldiers

refugee—a person fleeing war or oppression

resolution—formal statement of a decision by a legislature

revolution—a fight against a system of government

siege—to surround an enemy and cut off supplies

skirmish—a short battle with few casualties

tariff—tax on goods entering or leaving a country

taxes—money collected by a government

Tories—Loyalists who supported the British government

traitor—someone who helps the enemy

treaty—a formal agreement between nations

Answer Key

Page 28
1. d
2. a
3. c
4. b
5. c
6. b
7. b
8. a
9. c
10. a

Page 29
1. b
2. c
3. c
4. d
5. c
6. c
7. a
8. d
9. b
10. b

Page 30
1. b
2. a
3. c
4. b
5. a
6. c
7. a
8. b
9. c
10. d

Page 31
1 b
2. c
3. a
4. b
5. a
6. a
7. b

8. c
9. a
10. b

Page 32
1. d
2. a
3. c
4. d
5. b
6. d
7. c
8. c
9. a
10. c

Page 33
1. b
2. c
3. d
4. a
5. b
6. d
7. a
8. d
9. b
10. b

Page 34
1. c
2. b
3. a
4. c
5. d
6. b
7. c
8. a
9. c
10. d

Page 37
1. j
2. f
3. a
4. h

5. i
6. c
7. d
8. l
9. r
10. b
11. m
12. n
13. q
14. e
15. o
16. s
17. t
18. p
19. k
20. g

Page 38
1. necessary, dissolve, assume, separate, station, easy, persons, themselves, most, distempers, color, favorite, music, mathematics
2. Answers will vary

Page 40
Answers will vary. Accept reasonable responses.

Page 46
1. Lucy cut her hair to get money.
2. Lucy s parents had her head shaved and would not let her wear a bonnet.
3. The Fitzgerald boys fell through the ice.
4. Soldiers lacked food, clothing, and supplies.
5. Papa was a cobbler.
6. Quakers were against the war because of their religious beliefs.
7. Sir Billy was General William Howe.

Answer Key *(cont.)*

Page 46 *(cont.)*

8. The British paid in silver coins and gold.
9. Baron von Steuben communicated through translators.
10. Martha Washington bought the wig.

Page 48

1. Patriots killed her father because he opposed the Revolution.
2. Chad died on a British prison ship.
3. She acted differently and lived alone.
4. She was accused of starting a fire.
5. The Lightfoot family
6. Sam was an unpredictable, dangerous man.
7. Some people thought she was a witch.
8. Answers will vary.

Page 49

Sam Adams

1. He planned the Boston Tea Party and gave the orders to go.
2. He escaped in a carriage.
3. John Adams
4. He was going to represent Boston, Massachusetts, at the Continental Congress.
5. John Adams
6. Sam's dog
7. He lost money in a bank the British closed.

Paul Revere

1. silversmith, rang the church bells, soldier, engraved portraits, produced bookplates, sold pictures, made picture frames, made hymnbooks, dentist, made artificial teeth, built a barn, dispatch rider, spy, express rider, printed paper money, set up a powder mill, made cannon, hardware store owner, foundry owner, made bells, made copper sheeting
2. 11 days
3. 16 children
4. spurs and cloth to muffle the boat oars; his dog brought the spurs, and a woman gave him her petticoat
5. 2 days and 3 nights
6. The British took his horse.

Page 60

1764–Currency Act
1765–Quartering Act
1776–*Common Sense*
1777–Princeton
1779–Vincennes
1779–Stony Point
1780–King's Mountain
1781–Articles of Confederation

Page 61

1. New Hampshire
2. Massachusetts
3. Rhode Island
4. Connecticut
5. New York
6. Pennsylvania
7. New Jersey
8. Delaware
9. Maryland
10. Virginia
11. North Carolina
12. South Carolina
13. Georgia

Page 62

1. Pennsylvania, 1777
2. Massachusetts, 1775
3. South Carolina, 1780
4. South Carolina, 1780
5. Massachusetts, 1775
6. South Carolina, 1781
7. North Carolina, 1781
8. South Carolina, 1780
9. Massachusetts, 1775
10. New York, 1776
11. New Jersey, 1778
12. New Jersey, 1777
13. New York, 1777
14. Georgia, 1778
15. New York, 1775
16. New Jersey, 1776
17. West, 1779
18. Virginia, 1781
19. Lexington
20. Yorktown
21. Saratoga